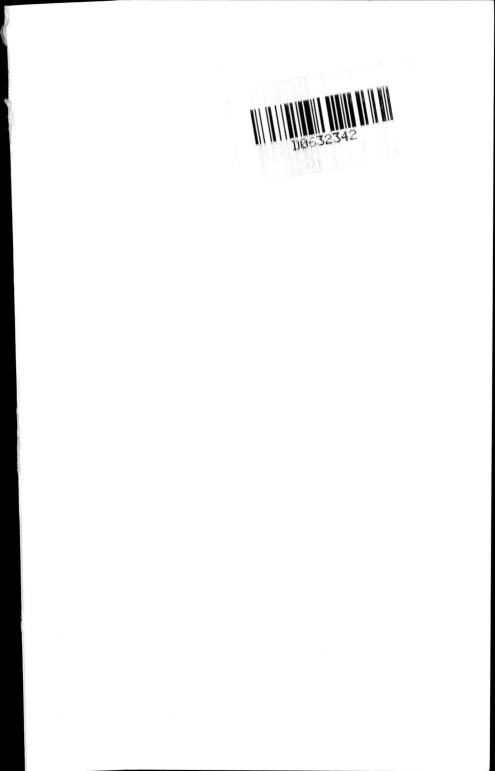

SOMETHING
NEEDS TO
CHANGE
AROUND
HERE

2ND EDITION

The Five Stages to Leveraging Your
LEADERSHIP

LIZ WEBER

The Five Stages of Focused Leadership Development™ and Necessary Conversations™ are pending trademarks of Liz Weber.

Cover design by Red Wolf Marketing
Radoma & Champoo8 Image(s) used under license from Shutterstock.com
Book design by Kate Rader

Published by Aspen Hill Press
2909 Conococheague Lane
Greencastle, PA 17225

This book is available at most online retailers.

**To order additional copies of this book, available in paperback
and e-book, or to order copies of this book in case lots,
visit www.WBSLLC.com**

Dedication

This book is dedicated to my parents, LeRoy and Frances Weber; my husband, Bob; my key team member, Gina; and my clients. Without my parents' examples of leadership, organization, and focus during my childhood, I wouldn't be able to do what I do for a living. Without Bob's stability and support, I wouldn't be able to relax at the end of the day or travel so comfortably and seamlessly to my clients. Without Gina's patience, dedication, and many skills, I'd be lost — let's just face it. And without my clients, there are far fewer sources of inspiration, opportunities to learn, or chances to work with incredible people and make a difference. **To all of you, thank you.**

Table of Contents

Preface » **So, what's new in this edition?**

In the years since the book was first released, I've had incredibly positive feedback from thousands of audience members and leadership training participants. Because of this feedback, we've developed the following materials and resources:

- **FREE Five Stages Leadership Assessment** — Available on our website, this free assessment quickly identifies which stage of leadership you are currently modeling. After you complete the assessment, you'll not only learn which stage of leadership you are modeling (and why you and your team may be experiencing the challenges you are experiencing), but you'll also receive free, virtual coaching insights to help you enhance your skills. These insights will help you identify and develop the critical skills you need so you can move to the next stage of leadership. Remember, when you move forward successfully, your team will too! Go to www. WBSLLC.com to take your free assessment.

- **Group and Individual Leadership Stage Reports** — Your entire leadership team can now take the FREE Five Stages Leadership Assessment too! When your team takes the assessment prior to one of my presentations, I'm able to customize my program to meet your team's specific leadership challenges. We're also able to offer you a Team Report, as well as Individual Reports for all your team members who took the assessment. These reports provide insight into how and where to focus your leadership team energies and how to better coach and support your individual managers. Go to www.WBSLLC.com for details.

· **Warning Signs Your Team Has Problems Moving Through The Five Stages of Focused Leadership Development™** — In this edition, I've included information on the Warning Signs to watch for in each stage of leadership. These warning signs are indicators to you that you or a team member is not moving through a stage of leadership smoothly. The challenge may be with one specific skill or it may be a combination of a few. Regardless, these warning signs are quick indicators that additional leadership focus and attention is required.

· **The Five Stages of Focused Leadership Development™ Facilitator Resources** — I am MOST excited to make these Facilitator Resources available to you! We've developed Facilitator Guides and Participant Materials so you can facilitate your own internal or client training. Simply follow the instructions and enjoy the conversations and learning that will follow. Information on these resources are in the new Section 3.

· **Discussion Questions for Management Teams or Book Clubs** — Discussion questions are included in the new Section 4. These questions have been developed so you can facilitate your own group discussions. These discussion questions are great for:

- Managers or Human Resources Professionals to use in facilitating Brown Bag Lunch discussions.
- Leadership team or Board of Director discussions on strategy, systems, efficiencies, depth and talent, trust, culture, change, organizational development, performance, engagement, succession, and board relationships, to name just a few.
- Book Clubs whose members have experience in management and leadership — or are seeking opportunities to manage and lead.

Thank you for your strong support of **The Five Stages of Focused Leadership Development**™ model and this book. I'm happy it's helped so many identify what they can do to become even better managers and leaders. As a result, they have grown to become the managers and leaders their teams need them to be.

I know you can too.

As noted in its original release, the names of many clients referenced in the book have been changed to maintain the confidentiality of our working relationships.

*If something
needs to change
around here,
it's probably you.*

SOMETHING NEEDS TO CHANGE AROUND HERE:

» The Five Stages to Leveraging Your Leadership

I knew from my initial telephone conversation with Dominic that he had been a successful CPA — in fact he had owned his own accounting practice for 27 years. However, he and Rose had purchased this small manufacturing firm five years prior and couldn't turn a profit. As I walked into Dominic's office, I could tell he was a numbers guy. There were financial statements, spreadsheets, and production run reports all over his desk. In fact, he needed to move a pile of papers from one of his office chairs just so I could sit down. Rose entered the office and looked tired. Dominic looked worn out too, so I wasn't surprised when he said, "Liz, I love to work, but I'm tired of working 50, 60, 70 or more hours a week. I'm tired of spending my nights and weekends here away from our family." Rose chimed in, "I'm tired of being handcuffed to this business! We're afraid to go on vacation for fear of what we'll find when we come back!" Dominic added, "I'm tired of being the only one who cares. Everyone brings their problems to me. They don't think. They don't figure things out for themselves. I'm starting to resent my employees and this business. Liz, something needs to change around here!"

I couldn't have agreed more. Something needed to change. But how could Dominic get his life back? He was the only person who knew his job and really knew this company. He was the owner and CEO. He was the one whose neck was on the line if things didn't get done. If you are a business owner, CEO, director, department head, or manager, how can you get your life back when you're handcuffed to it? As I walk you through **The Five Stages of Focused Leadership Development**™, you'll identify how you can change the way you behave and the way you lead, so you're no longer resentful of the people with whom you work, you're no longer playing catch-up just to keep up, and you'll identify obvious ways you too can get your life back.

You see, as Dominic shared a bit more about his business, it soon became clear to me there were obvious changes that needed to occur. So, in my ever-so-subtle way, I said, "Dominic, you're right. Something does need to change around here: You."

If you're in a leadership position and you walk around complaining to others or saying to yourself, "Something needs to change around here," you're right. And the first thing that needs to change is you. You need to learn to do your job better because you're not doing it right or well now. The typical reason for this is: **You don't understand what your real job as a manager or leader is.**

Most managers and leaders are under incredible amounts of pressure to perform. Yet much of the pressure is self-imposed. It's a result of being so busy being busy, they're not doing what they're really supposed to do. It's a result of not understanding what their real roles and responsibilities are as managers and leaders. It's a result of confusing Doing with Managing or Leading. And it's a result of them continuing to work the way they always have: Keep my head down and plow ahead. However, because of this, there are now rivers of confusion, frustration, and stress throughout the organization. Employees are working frantically, expediting orders, and working around inefficient processes and unresolved problems. When asked, no one — including the managers and leaders — can concisely state what they're all working toward; they're just busy trying to stay afloat.

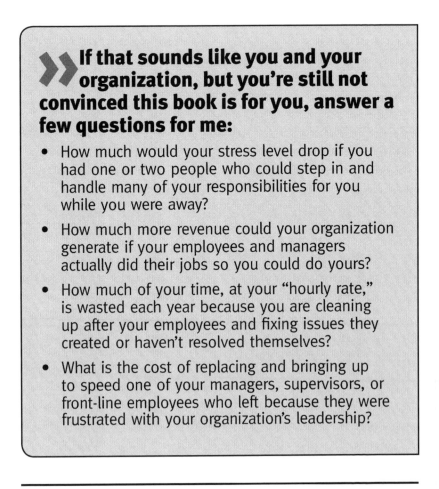

If that sounds like you and your organization, but you're still not convinced this book is for you, answer a few questions for me:

- How much would your stress level drop if you had one or two people who could step in and handle many of your responsibilities for you while you were away?

- How much more revenue could your organization generate if your employees and managers actually did their jobs so you could do yours?

- How much of your time, at your "hourly rate," is wasted each year because you are cleaning up after your employees and fixing issues they created or haven't resolved themselves?

- What is the cost of replacing and bringing up to speed one of your managers, supervisors, or front-line employees who left because they were frustrated with your organization's leadership?

Did your answers make you sit back and think a bit? If you're like many managers and leaders, they probably did. Don't feel bad if your answers made you a bit nervous. These are the same questions I ask my clients, and their answers usually make them nervous too. When I asked Dominic these questions, he didn't answer them. He just stared at me with an "Oh crap!" look on his face.

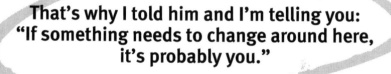

That's why I told him and I'm telling you: "If something needs to change around here, it's probably you."

Now don't be offended. I'm simply stating a reality I (and others) see. That's my job. I point out to my consulting and coaching clients the reality and the consequences of their actions when their team members are afraid to or don't see them. Why do I do this? As a manager or leader, when you are aware of and are no longer embarrassed by your leadership weaknesses and their real and negative impact on your team and your organization,

you're positioned to change your thinking and your behaviors. You're then better able to do your job and fulfill
your role and responsibilities as a leader. You're better
able to become the leader others need you to be. When
you do that, you're able to help your teams and employees
perform more effectively. Simply put, when you do your
job better, you're in a better position to help your employees perform theirs better too.

If you'd like to learn which of **The Five Stages of
Focused Leadership Development**™ you are currently
modeling, go to www.WBSLLC.com and take our Free
Five Stages Assessment.

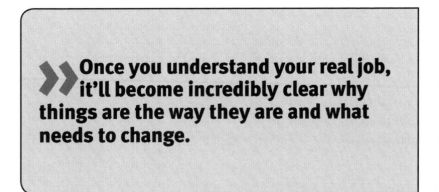

**Once you understand your real job,
it'll become incredibly clear why
things are the way they are and what
needs to change.**

Simply put,
when you do your job
better, you are in a
better position
to help your employees
perform theirs
better too.

"For most employees, your title doesn't matter. Many people with important sounding titles can't manage, and even more fall short when it comes to leading. Employees don't care about your title; they care about what you do."
—Liz Weber

SECTION 1

WHAT IS YOUR REAL JOB?

"JUST BECAUSE YOU HAVE THE TITLE 'MANAGER' OR 'LEADER,' IT DOESN'T MEAN YOU CAN LEAD."

—LIZ WEBER

What Is Your Job — Really?

So, what is your job — really? I know that may sound like a rather in-sulting question, but honestly, it's THE question I help my clients answer. Until they can answer that question, they often struggle as managers and leaders. Until you know the answer to that question as soon as you hear it, you'll struggle as a manager and leader too.

In reality, the answer to this question is not as simple as you might think. Other than what is assumed of you because of your title or what is listed in your position description, you may not understand what you're really supposed to be doing at work. To clarify this seemingly basic — but critically important — question, let me first clarify what I consider a job to be. Then I'll outline the basic leadership hierarchy and core jobs found in typical organizations. Finally, I'll clarify what the real job of a manager or a leader is, and I'll clarify how you may have missed the mark in doing your job — your *real* job.

First, a job is more than a snazzy title. It's a combination of the role(s) you are expected to perform within the organization (or in a specific team) and the responsibilities you are expected to cover (again, within the organization or in a specific team).

In this book, I refer to these two elements as your job, with the understanding that on any given day, your role and responsibilities shift — even though your title stays the same. Effective managers and leaders know this. Effective managers and leaders constantly flex their focus and behaviors given the needs of the teams, customers, organization, and industry. Ineffective managers and leaders get stuck because of their job titles. They focus on what they believe their job is — given their title — instead of what their job really is. As a result, they behave in ways that hinder success — their own, their team's, and their organization's.

Second, even though there are many who profess the benefits of organic, non-structured organizations, the fact is, effective organizations have structure. Some organizations require high levels of structure, others less, but there is structure and a rhyme and reason to how every effective organization operates. The most basic element of an effective organization's structure is establishing and understanding its hierarchy.

›› Commonly, organizations have the following structure:

- Board of Directors
- CEO/President
- Managers (Middle Management to Vice Presidents)
- Managers/Front-line Supervisors/Project Managers
- Front-line Staff

This simple structure supports a basic separation of jobs. It breaks down the roles and responsibilities within the organization. It enables the organization to have people performing the hands-on work of the organization, others coordinating those efforts, and still others planning for the organization's future. Everyone has roles and responsibilities to cover. When all employees do their jobs by ful-filling their roles and responsibilities completely, things move along relatively smoothly. However, when people don't do their jobs, when roles and responsibilities are not fulfilled as they need to be, confusion and frustration ensue. Problems arise. Follow-through doesn't occur. Communication gaps widen. Accountability lapses increase. Rumors and finger-pointing abound. Departmental silos deepen. Now here's the reality my clients don't want to hear: managers and leaders cause most of the organizational confusion and frustration by not doing their jobs — their real jobs.

To get a sense of what each organizational level's true job is, let's review the following organizational hierarchy from front-line staff up to the board of directors. As we work from bottom to top, I'll introduce **The Five Stages of Focused Leadership Development**™ model. I have enhanced and used this model for years as a tool to help supervisors, managers, CEOs, owners, and boards of directors understand the importance of doing the jobs they're supposed to be doing. It takes the basic "Doing to Managing" model and expands upon it. **The Five Stages of Focused Leadership Development**™ model explains what it takes to be an effective leader to best support the team and the organization. **The Five Stages of Focused Leadership Development**™ model is simple. Through the years, it has helped my clients understand how to change themselves so they can develop their teams and, subsequently, help their organizations move forward. I believe it can help you too.

The Five Stages of
Focused Leadership Development™

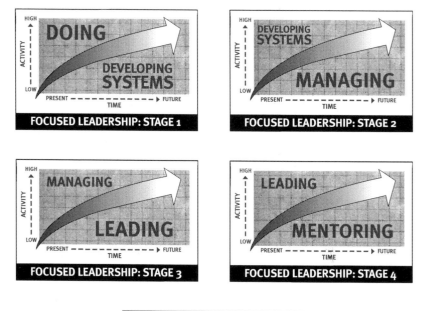

The Five Stages of Focused Leadership Development™ Model

As I share **The Five Stages of Focused Leadership Development**™, you will probably see yourself at various times in one if not many of the stages. In fact, you will probably say to yourself, "On any given day, I'm in all of these stages!" That's normal. Depending upon the day, you may be in Stage 1 as you work closely with select team members to develop the scope and expectations for a new strategic initiative. That same day, you may spend hours in a strategic planning session debating your organization's future. Then you wrap up your day by having dinner with fellow board members from a charity you support as an advisory board member on leadership succession. Every effective leader flexes and moves each and every day.

The key is to ensure you are at any point in time leading from the stage your team and organization needs.To help you determine this, let's work through The Five Stages of Focused Leadership Development™.

The following five models all follow the same format. In the Stage 1 model, "DOING" decreases and "DEVELOPING SYSTEMS" increases over time. With each model, the horizontal axis illustrates the progression of time — Present to the Future as you move from left to right. The vertical axis illustrates the amount of activity you dedicate to each of the two responsibilities identified in each diagram — from Low to High. As you move from left to right (toward the Future) on the model, the behavior in the upper wedge diminishes, and the behavior in the lower wedge increases. Basically, each model indicates that over time, if you focus on and act to purposely develop your leadership skills, you will start to demonstrate more of the behaviors in the lower wedge and fewer of the behaviors in the upper wedge.

Keep in mind, even if you master the skills in all five stages, there is no stage that is better or worse than the others. If you are truly an effective leader, you will flex and move throughout the stages depending upon where your team needs you at any given point in time.

You may well be a seasoned, experienced executive who has built several successful teams and organizations. However, when you take over a new division with the expectation that you will turn it around, you may well have to back-up and get very 'hands-on' with Stage 1 Leadership behaviors. These behaviors will allow you to work with your new team in identifying system failures. However, as your new team starts to make progress in identifying and refining systems, you start to back out of Stage 1 and model more Stage 2 Leadership behaviors. As your new managers take on their management roles more competently, you move to Stage 3 Leadership behaviors. When your management team is clear and aligned with you in where the division is headed over the next three or more years, you help them identify ways to enhance the skills and depth of your workforce. You model Stage 4 Leadership. Finally, when you've developed a solid leadership team of your own that is consistently developing and supporting their teams, you again look to Move On. You become a Stage 5 Leader again.

Do you want to be a leader?

STAGE 1

Transition from Doing to Developing Systems

Let's get started. To help you visualize what each stage looks like in the workplace, I'll share some examples with you.

> **THE COMPLACENCY EFFECT:**
> **Spotting Trouble in the Development**
> **of Stage 1 Leadership**

The easiest way to identify limited or weak Stage 1 Leadership skills in employees is to review the words used to describe the individuals. If words such as go-getters, smart, savvy, leaders, or creative are used, you've probably got some strong Stage 1 Leadership candidates. However, words such as lazy, apathetic, entitled, uncaring, or complacent describe individuals with limited or as yet hidden Stage 1 Leadership behaviors.

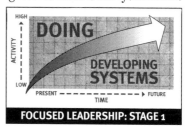

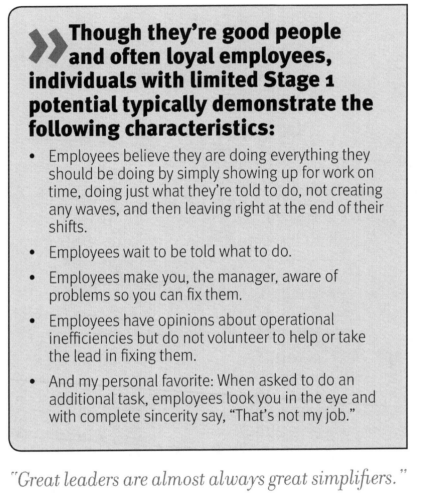

➤➤ Though they're good people and often loyal employees, individuals with limited Stage 1 potential typically demonstrate the following characteristics:

- Employees believe they are doing everything they should be doing by simply showing up for work on time, doing just what they're told to do, not creating any waves, and then leaving right at the end of their shifts.

- Employees wait to be told what to do.

- Employees make you, the manager, aware of problems so you can fix them.

- Employees have opinions about operational inefficiencies but do not volunteer to help or take the lead in fixing them.

- And my personal favorite: When asked to do an additional task, employees look you in the eye and with complete sincerity say, "That's not my job."

"Great leaders are almost always great simplifiers."
— General Colin Powell

As frustrating as these behaviors can be, we've all worked with individuals who demonstrate them. Ironically, many of these individuals wonder why they don't get promoted or get asked to be a part of creative teams. Well, there are several reasons, but the one I'll focus on here is: they don't demonstrate Stage 1 Leadership thinking or action.

So, what is Stage 1 Leadership?

Stage 1 is where you started your professional career. When you started to work, you were probably a front-line worker. You were "a doer." You were the individual inputting the data, doing the fieldwork, serving the customers, making the widgets, or in some other way doing the work for which the organization was known. You were a part of the front-line staff. Then over time, you demonstrated you liked to learn and improve things. You became adept at your job, and you started to think of ways you could do your job more efficiently. You developed ways to do your job more systematically so you wouldn't have to re-create the wheel every time you came to work. You started to create shortcuts, checklists, procedures, and standards to help you do your job quickly, consistently, and efficiently. You started to develop systems. These new systems would help you do good work with less effort. They also served as a way for

*By identifying a need and then taking
the initiative to create systems to improve how
you worked, you were demonstrating
Stage 1 Leadership thinking and behaviors.*

you to identify and document the best practices for many of the tasks you were responsible for or those that impacted you. These systems and standards were one way to solve problems, streamline processes, and create organization. These systems would also free you up to do more challenging things because you were starting to outgrow your current front-line job. And honestly, you were starting to get bored with your current role and responsibilities. You were looking for ways to free up some of your time so you could do other, more challenging things.

When these thoughts and actions occurred, you, like many other prospective managers and leaders, took the first step of **The Five Stages of Focused Leadership Development**™. You understood the value of creating and leveraging systems to get things done. By identifying a need and then taking the initiative to create systems to improve how you worked, you were demonstrating Stage 1 Leadership thinking and behaviors. You understood that the purpose of developing organizational standards and systems is to enhance workflow and gain consistency. Systems would help grow the business.

Systems Increase Your Value

By developing systems as a Stage 1 Leader, you not only increased your individual value to the organization, but you also increased the organization's value. Your individual value was enhanced as you demonstrated to others your ability to create organization and systems where none existed before. And by taking this first step of **The Five Stages of Focused Leadership Development**™, you showed your managers and others your skills in problem solving and creating instructions and guides to help others. You became more valuable to the organization as you were viewed as a candidate to fix other jobs where there was a lack of consistency, efficiency, and organization. You started to position yourself as a problem solver (or special projects person) whether you intended to or not.

Who knew that by you doing your job better and more efficiently, you would help others to do theirs better as well?

Also, the initial individual benefit you antici-pated from creating systems was more far reaching than you had expected. By creating systems for your own use, you had, by default, created quality control, performance management, training and production aids, or some other type of system for others who may be asked to do your job or similar jobs. Current and future employees would need to know how and why certain things are done the way they are. You created aids and tools that could be used when you were on vacation or had moved on to other duties. You developed systems that would help other employees do their jobs.

The documented systems increase the organization's value to potential purchasers as there are now "instructions" on how to run the business.

Systems Create Value for the Organization

From the organization's perspective, these tools, these systems, create value: when key organizational systems and processes are documented, the company's value increases. The documented systems increase the organization's value to potential purchasers as there are now "instructions" on how to run the business. The organization becomes less dependent upon select knowledgeable individuals and more dependent upon employees who can understand, use, and enhance the systems already in place.

One of my clients, a small professional cleaning franchise, experienced the power of having documented business processes and systems in place. I've worked with this client on various projects over the years, and during our first year working together, I had pushed the management team to document operational and administrative systems and procedures. I told them by developing and documenting their systems, they would realize several benefits.

⟫ Developing Systems will:

1. Clarify who should be doing what and why.

By reviewing processes (critical first and then others), the management team and staff will be forced to review: Who does what, why, and how? This activity alone will generate conversations and debates on why certain individuals are doing, or not doing, certain tasks and why some processes are the way they are. Obvious realignments to get the right people doing the right tasks can then be made, and needed process improvements will be identified.

2. Create instructional aids for use in training new and cross-training current staff.

3. Create standards (performance or production) to enhance consistency.

4. Create a tangible asset for the company and increase the company's value.

James, the company's president, readily saw the value of those first three points but wasn't sold on the fourth point — until they'd loaded the documented procedures into one database. This new data center suddenly allowed current, consistent, and correct files to be accessed by appropriate staff from any workstation, and it eliminated the need to swap out or update old paper copies of forms and procedures from various posted locations and binders throughout their facilities. When James saw his staff using the new system, he called me: "I can't believe how valuable this system is! This is essentially the instruction manual on how to run this business. If I were to sell this business, all I'd need to do was show the buyer this set of files and say, 'Here are the keys.'"

About two years after this insight, James was presented with an opportunity to purchase a competitor. If all went well, this purchase alone would quadruple their base of operations and potentially quadruple sales within a few years. As James and his team conducted their due diligence, the potential purchase looked more and more promising. It wouldn't be easy, but there were no major surprises. The competitor was larger, and had a fairly well-run business, but it was not as well organized or operationally efficient as my client's firm. Now here's the fun part: after completing his due diligence, James told me, "We're going to buy this company. They're much larger, but we have all the systems. We're simply going to expand our systems and use them as templates to take over and enhance operations in our new markets. We'll orient and train the new staff in the same way we trained our current staff."

They did, and within one year they had realized a fairly seamless business expansion. By utilizing only the necessary infrastructure systems to enhance operations and communications, they brought the larger organization online. The experience wasn't stress-free for management or the staff of either organization. However, my client was able to clearly communicate and show the new team what systems were going to be implemented, why, and how. This helped to minimize the confusion and anxiety of the new staff and gave James's management team tangible tools to use in orienting and training new staff. The systems worked.

Don't Underestimate the Power of Developing Systems

So what could happen if you don't develop systems? Well, nothing will change, you'll continue to do it all and be it all, and you'll continue to feel handcuffed to your job.

That may sound a bit dramatic, so let me share some specific consequences with you:

1. You remain the default problem solver.

If you're the primary person who resolves customer issues, tweaks the equipment, realigns production schedules, or whatever it is you do, who will your team members go to when something goes wrong? You. Why? Because when they do, you solve the problems for them. Now here's the interesting part: you do these things because, on the surface, it seems the most efficient way to handle them.

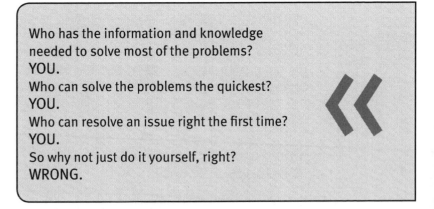

Who has the information and knowledge needed to solve most of the problems?
YOU.
Who can solve the problems the quickest?
YOU.
Who can resolve an issue right the first time?
YOU.
So why not just do it yourself, right?
WRONG.

If it's a problem that falls within their scope of work responsibilities, your team members should be fixing them.

Do not let one-deep scenarios hold your business hostage. Develop systems.

If you don't get yourself out of this cycle, you'll end up coming to work an hour or two early to work on management things. Then you will spend the bulk of the work day resolving issues for your team. At the end of the day, your team members will leave, but you will stay an hour or two to work on management things that didn't get done all day long — because you weren't doing your job, you were doing your team's! You need to do your job; they need to do theirs.

2. You remain overly dependent upon select staff.

Consider this: People leave. People die. People forget. In working with clients on leadership succession, my mantra is: **Never put your business in the hands of one person or a select few. Why? People leave. People die. People forget.** Protect your business by creating systems that can be shared with others; transferred from person to person, team to team, or facility to facility; and accessed from virtually anywhere. Why? I've seen it happen too many times: The one employee who was the heart and soul of the department or business leaves unexpectedly, and the organization's leaders go into shock and then panic mode:

How could she leave us? Karen handled everything?

No one else knows Karen's job!

How do we check a customer's order? How do we log on to Karen's system?

After the shock and panic start to fade, the leaders realize their ability to operate the business is restricted because the one person who left was the only person who knew how to handle critical issues and processes. Now their operations and customers are negatively impacted because one person left the organization. That's wrong. They may well blame Karen for leaving, but it's not Karen's fault. It's theirs. The leaders weren't doing their jobs. They weren't developing an organization by ensuring systems were in place to prevent situations like this from happening.

I'll say it again: Never put your business in the hands of one person or a select few. People leave. People die. People forget.

Do not let the one-deep scenarios (i.e., only one employee knows how to do a critical process) hold your business hostage. Develop systems.

3. You miss opportunities to enhance efficiencies.

As mentioned earlier, other consequences of not requiring systems development are the missed opportunities to challenge your management team and employees to think about how and why they do what they do, and then to benefit by what their thinking reveals.

>> By challenging everyone to reassess what, how, and why they do what they do...

You will cause employees to analyze their current roles and responsibilities.

- Ask your employees to specify: Who is doing what and why? Why is this person doing that task?
- This often reveals that many team members are doing certain tasks simply because they've always done them, even though other people (holding other positions) should be doing them.

You will cause employees to analyze their current processes and systems.

- Ask your employees to specify for each process and system: Why is this done that way? Is it efficient this way, or does it cause frustrations or problems for others? How can it be done more simply and with fewer steps?
- This often highlights many processes that are done a certain way because that's how they've "always" been done — even though it's no longer the most efficient method.

You will promote knowledge sharing and deepen the skill sets of your employees.

- Ask your employees: Who else knows how to do this? Who can fill in for you when you're out? Every person, and I do mean every person, should have a backup — either a person or system in place that others can access — to keep things going while she or he is away.

> *"Systems create freedom."*
> *—Neen James*

Create Systems and Tools, Not Just a Bunch of Paperwork

In his classic, mega-hit book, *The E-Myth*, Michael E. Gerber shares the importance of creating and leveraging simple systems. I want to highlight that point here. Any of the systems (i.e., checklists, processes, procedures, etc.) you create must be simple and easy. That's why the tricky part to developing systems is to ensure you're not creating a rigid bureaucracy. Don't document everything just for the sake of having documentation.

>> Develop simple, effective systems first. Then document them. Here's how:

Document and communicate what isn't obvious to others.

- What are your primary job responsibilities?
- What do you handle that no one else may be aware of?
- What project background or history may be helpful for others to know?
- Document and communicate those critical tasks you do that — if you're not around and they don't get done — cause bottlenecks for co-workers or customers.
- What tasks are critical to the business?
- What do you do that others depend upon in order to do their work?
- What do you do that directly affects your customers that no one else does?
- What issues are unique to a customer, machine, etc.?
- What do you know how to do that no one else does?
- What do you know how to access or fix that no one else does?
- What adds value for the customer that no one else may know?

"Be a yardstick of quality.
Some people aren't used to an
environment where excellence is expected."
—Steve Jobs

If your organization is missing a systems infrastructure, focus your energies on establishing standards for performance and production. Then focus on reviewing, refining, and then documenting the critical procedures (i.e., those that directly impact others). Keep in mind, developing the systems is only the start. For the systems to work and be effective over the long term, they need to be reviewed, revised, and updated regularly. As W.E. Deming said, "Eighty-five percent of all failure is in the system." If the system isn't working, fix it. A solid Stage 1 Leader will help identify and provide fixes when they're needed.

Several years ago I received my electric bill and noticed an incorrect charge. I called the utility company's service center to have them remove the charge. After being placed on hold for several minutes, a very nice woman came on the telephone to help me. I gave her my account number and explained the reason for my call.

What she said next amazed me. "These issues are handled by our Nebraska service center. The woman there who can fix this is out today. They had some nasty tornadoes go through there last night and she lost the roof of her house. She'll be back in later this week." What amazed me wasn't her honesty in sharing a personal tragedy affecting one of her colleagues — and believe me, I felt bad for her colleague. What amazed me was there was only one woman in their entire service center who had the skills or authority to fix my incorrect bill! I wasn't asking them to design a new utility grid for my neighborhood; I was simply asking for an incorrect charge to be removed from my bill. Yet only one person knew how to do that. They obviously had skimped on developing and sharing a process to address incorrect charges!

You Too Can Delegate

Now you may be thinking, "Well this is all fine and dandy, but I don't have anyone to whom I can delegate. Why should I bother developing systems?" Why indeed. Actually, that's a great question and exactly where many doers with leadership potential mess up. They don't believe this first stage or first step in leadership development applies to them because they're not leading anyone yet or they're a one-person business.

»If you're the only person who does your job and will be the only person to be doing your job in the foreseeable future, let me ask you a few questions...

If you own your own business:

- Do you ever go on vacation?
- Are you ever sick, have to take a family member to the doctor, or have you ever been unable to come to work?
- Do you ever have more work to do than you can handle at any one time?
- Have you ever thought, "If I were to sell my business next year, what would the buyer be buying?"

If you're an employee working for another organization:

- Do you ever go on vacation?
- Are you ever sick, have to take a family member to the doctor, or have you ever been unable to come to work?
- Do you ever have more work to do than you can handle at any one time?

*Wake up!
Everyone can
be replaced.*

If any of these situations have ever happened to you, what happens to your tasks while you're away? Nothing. Right. Or, if you're part of a multi-person organization, have you ever had the experience that even though you're supposed to be on vacation, your phone rings constantly because your co-workers can't figure out how you do what you do so they can do what they need to do while you're away? As their calls come in do you roll your eyes, wonder how they function in the other aspects of their life without you, and then, out of the goodness of your heart, tell them what to do? Or, do you tell them you'll handle everything when you get back to work?

If this scenario sounds like you, let me tell you something: Quit feeling so important! You're a control freak who doesn't think anyone else can do your job! Wake up! Everyone can be replaced. However, until you realize that and stop trying to control everything, you will continue to create an environment where people are dependent upon you — even though you get irritated because they are dependent upon you! Now that's just twisted, isn't it? So if you're frequently frustrated because you spend much of your time fixing problems, you need to create systems for anything that needs to get done that impacts others.

If you're frustrated by what your team members don't know or can't figure out, help them. Develop processes, checklists, instructions. Develop systems.

Be an Effective Stage 1 Leader: Don't Just Share, Train Too

As a Stage 1 Leader, you understand that by developing systems for your individual use, you help yourself and you help others. However, be fair about sharing the information. Be realistic. Don't assume because you tell your co-workers where your procedural checklists are located, they'll remember or even have a clue what to do with the lists if they happen to find them. Take the time to show your co-workers where procedures and lists are located; how to access them; and how to actually do what's documented. Don't simply tell them, "The procedures are in the main systems files!" as you run to catch the plane to Margaritaville. For any critical process you perform, document it. Then, have your co-workers practice accessing the procedures and following them as you watch and coach them. Do a test run or two with any colleagues who will be filling in for you while you're away.

Backfill to move on.

   A practical and obvious time to conduct these 'test runs' is before you take your vacation or

any planned leave. In the week or two prior to you taking your leave, take time to teach your critical tasks and responsibilities to your colleagues. Let them practice. Help them get comfortable and ask questions while you're still available. If they need to call you while you are away to ask where to find something or how to do a task, it's not a sign you are invaluable. It's an indication you didn't train them well enough.

You've created great training and learning tools for yourself and others, so take the final step as a Stage 1 Leader and teach others how to use them. Backfill so you can move on. Share what you've created so others can do the work. Then you can actually go on vacation, relax, and enjoy your margarita(s) in peace. Now, wouldn't that be a great way to start to get your life back?

>> Warning Signs You or a Team Member is Having Problems Behaving as a Stage 1 Leader:

- You believe simply showing up for work on time, doing only what is asked of you, not creating any waves, and then leaving right at the end of your shift is enough.

- You wait for your manager to tell you what to do.

- You make your manager aware of problems so she or he will fix them.

- You have strong opinions about operational inefficiencies and ideas on how to fix them, but you do not volunteer to help or take the lead in fixing them.

- And my personal favorite: When your manager asks to do an additional task, you respond by saying, "That's not my job."

Any or all of the above behaviors indicate a failure on the leadership team's part to create a culture that expects and encourages all employees to understand: They matter. Every employee is hired with the expectation that she or he will pay attention to the work they do. All employees need to understand the importance of the work they do, regardless of position or title. And all employees need to feel comfortable in knowing they are expected and encouraged to look for ways to improve what they do so they can help their organization perform better and thereby support their clients, customers, members, or guests better.

Not every suggestion or potential enhancement will be a success. But every suggestion or enhancement was generated because someone identified an opportunity and acted upon it. That's what Stage 1 Leaders do.

>> Keys to Stage 1 Leadership:

- Doers with leadership potential demonstrate Stage 1 Leadership behaviors when they identify ways to do their jobs more efficiently and then create systems to help get things done.

- Doers become more valuable to the organization when they create systems to replace confusion and a lack of consistency, efficiency, and organization.

- Systems add value to the organization by creating instructions on how to run operations, as well as to serve as training aids for other staff.

- Systems should be easy, and they should be clear. They should be helpful tools, not a bureaucracy of documentation.

- Stage 1 Leaders train others how to access and use their systems to keep things going while they're away. Leaders backfill and move on.

Why is being a manager so hard?

STAGE 2

Transition from Developing Systems to Managing

You've been promoted!
You're now the manager.
So why isn't your team productive?

> **THE BOTTLENECK EFFECT:**
> Spotting Trouble in the Transition
> to Stage 2 Leadership

One of the most blatant signs a manager has failed to make the transition to Stage 2 Leadership is that even though she's been promoted to a management position, she continues to do the work her team members (i.e., the Doers) are supposed to be doing. When that happens, teams, departments, and entire organizations have limited performance potential because there's only so much one manager can do!

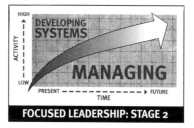

FOCUSED LEADERSHIP: STAGE 2

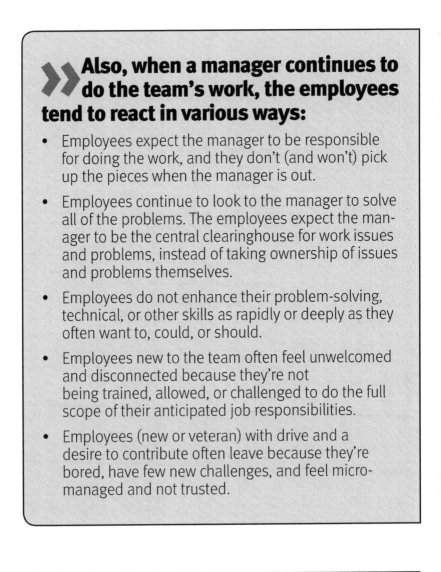

>> Also, when a manager continues to do the team's work, the employees tend to react in various ways:

- Employees expect the manager to be responsible for doing the work, and they don't (and won't) pick up the pieces when the manager is out.

- Employees continue to look to the manager to solve all of the problems. The employees expect the manager to be the central clearinghouse for work issues and problems, instead of taking ownership of issues and problems themselves.

- Employees do not enhance their problem-solving, technical, or other skills as rapidly or deeply as they often want to, could, or should.

- Employees new to the team often feel unwelcomed and disconnected because they're not being trained, allowed, or challenged to do the full scope of their anticipated job responsibilities.

- Employees (new or veteran) with drive and a desire to contribute often leave because they're bored, have few new challenges, and feel micromanaged and not trusted.

A manager has failed to achieve Stage 2 Leadership when she continues to do the work her team members are supposed to be doing.

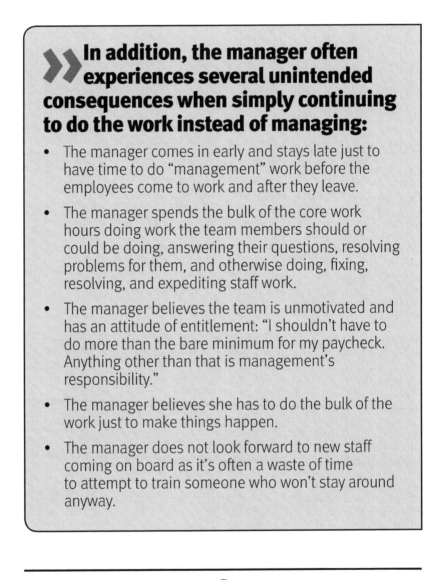

» In addition, the manager often experiences several unintended consequences when simply continuing to do the work instead of managing:

- The manager comes in early and stays late just to have time to do "management" work before the employees come to work and after they leave.

- The manager spends the bulk of the core work hours doing work the team members should or could be doing, answering their questions, resolving problems for them, and otherwise doing, fixing, resolving, and expediting staff work.

- The manager believes the team is unmotivated and has an attitude of entitlement: "I shouldn't have to do more than the bare minimum for my paycheck. Anything other than that is management's responsibility."

- The manager believes she has to do the bulk of the work just to make things happen.

- The manager does not look forward to new staff coming on board as it's often a waste of time to attempt to train someone who won't stay around anyway.

- The manager regularly tells herself: "I'll just handle it myself. That way I don't have to deal with their complaints, whining, or rationalizations as to why they don't know how to do the work."

- The manager firmly believes she is the only one who cares and that she does more work than anyone on the team.

- The manager always seems be digging through the bottleneck of work piling up for her to handle.

As a manager, if you experience any or all of the above, you are not alone. The overwhelming majority of managers who take my free Five Stages Leadership Assessment, fall into Stage 2 Leadership, and it indicates it's time for them to change. Like them, you are not doing, or not yet doing, your job — your real job. By understanding the benefits of effective Stage 2 Leadership, you can avoid these long-term, dysfunctional workplace consequences. You will enhance your productivity, reduce your frustration, and improve your working relationships — just by doing your job and by ensuring your team members are doing the jobs they're being paid to do.

Great Stage 1 Leaders Don't Necessarily Make Great Stage 2 Leaders

Many organizations and individuals get into trouble attempting Stage 2 Leadership when the time isn't right. The problems arise because, more often than not, organizations promote the most technically proficient doers into supervisory, team leader, or management roles. However, a great Stage 1 Leader doesn't necessarily make a great Stage 2 Leader.

"We teach people how to treat us."
—Dr. Phil McGraw

>> **The skills needed to be an effective supervisor, team leader, or manager are vastly different from those needed to be a proficient doer.**

Doers are the front-line, hands-on, do-the-work people. They're usually responsible for their individual output and for their specific, defined responsibilities. Effective doers utilize systems and processes to help them do their jobs, but they still do the work themselves. Supervisors and managers, on the other hand, use the systems and processes to leverage and coordinate the work of many doers and thereby enhance the individual team member and unified team efforts. Supervisors and managers also are responsible for ensuring the work of the various doers is getting done

on time, within budget, and in accordance with quality and customer specifications. Managers drive productivity and efficiency. Managers are responsible for ensuring the organization's resources (i.e., people, materials, facilities, money, etc.) are being utilized most effectively, here and now, to meet the organization's near-term goals and objectives.

Promote with Purpose

Even though great doers often lack the interpersonal, communication, multi-tasking, and organization skills needed by effective supervisors and managers, upper management continues to promote the most technically competent doers because they're the best! Right? As Marcus Buckingham and Curt Coffman state sarcastically in *First, Break All The Rules,* "We still think that the most creative way to reward excellence in a role is to promote the person out of it."

If we want great people in management, does it make sense to promote the best doer? Not necessarily.

»There are several reasons why promoting doers into management roles doesn't always work.

First, the most-used skills of effective managers are their communication skills. Effective doers utilize systems and processes to help them do their jobs, but they still do the work themselves.

Supervisors and managers, on the other hand, use the systems and processes to leverage and coordinate the work of many doers and thereby enhance the individual team member and unified team efforts. Supervisors and managers also are responsible for ensuring the work of the various doers is getting done on time, within budget, and in accordance with quality and customer specifications. Managers drive productivity and efficiency. Managers are responsible for ensuring the organization's resources (i.e., people, materials, facilities, money, etc.) are being utilized most effectively, here and now, to meet the organization's near-term goals and objectives.

Second, after they promote the most proficient doer, management is often surprised to see production numbers drop. They become frustrated with the new manager. He used to be a star performer but now he

can't perform in this job. What did management expect? They just took the top producer off the line! The remaining team has weaker skills, yet they're expected to produce as much if not more than before. So to help his team meet their production requirements, the newly promoted manager falls into a common trap. He'll continue to do a good bit of the hands-on technical work, and he'll work his heart out to perform his new management tasks too. This works fine in the short term, but in the longer term he'll become a burnt-out, disenfranchised manager.

Third, many proficient doers simply do not want supervisory or management responsibilities. They're completely happy being a Stage 1 Leader. They know if they accept a promotion they will have to change how they work, think, and communicate to do their new jobs well. However, they understand themselves and their work preferences. They like to work the way they currently do. They're happy being Stage 1 Leaders. Therefore, it doesn't work for them, you, or the team if you try to force them into an unhappy Stage 2 Leadership position.

Any one of the above scenarios is tough for the new manager. However, for some reason upper management continues to expect exceptional doers to somehow morph into exceptional managers, and that's just not fair or realistic.

Pinpoint Stage 2 Potential

➤➤So what should you consider before thrusting the exceptional doer into a sink-or-swim management position?

First, watch and assess the doer's interpersonal, communication, organizational, and systems develop-ment skills — not just his technical skills.

Second, give the exceptional doer a few opportunities to test and develop his supervisory or management skills before thrusting him into the role officially. Coach him, and then have him run a team meeting or two to gauge his skill in communicating with his peers and coordinating their actions. Coach him, and then have him be responsible for explaining to the team the benefits of implementing new systems and their impact on efficiencies. Coach him, and then have him take the lead on a project or two.

Help your Stage 1 Leader, your exceptional doer, realize his own potential to move to Stage 2 if he hasn't seen it for himself. Let him start to consider and warm up to the idea of a shift in his role and responsibilities. If you gauge your Stage 1 Leader's desire and ability to transition

The hardest thing for most managers to learn is: Let go! However, if you don't let go, others can't do!

mentally from doing to managing before abruptly moving him, you'll increase the likelihood he'll be ready to move physically as he will have already started to shift mentally to Stage 2 thinking. Similarly, if you have a Stage 1 Leader who wants to move up, assess his skills. He might not be ready yet. He might need to be coached a bit more in the basic skills of Stage 2 Leadership. Think before you promote. Ensure you're creating an environment for everyone to succeed: your new Stage 2 Leader, the team, and your organization.

Stop Doing and Start Managing: Backfill to Move On

Once you, the efficient doer, have started to make the mental shift from doing to managing and are officially moved into your new role as manager, you have to stop doing the work! I know that's terribly difficult for you because you are the most proficient doer and you probably helped create the systems, policies, and procedures in the first place. Besides let's be honest, who's still the best doer? You! Who can still do the task the quickest? You! Who can get it right the first time? You! And therein lies the problem, as well as the key to a successful evolution through **The Five Stages of Focused Leadership Development**™. The hardest thing for most managers to learn is: Let go! You need to learn to let go of what you know how

*Learn to trust others to have the right skills
and abilities. Learn to delegate.
Learn to verify results.
Learn to support. Learn to let go.*

to do well so others can learn to do it. If you don't
let go, others can't do.

To effectively move yourself from one leadership stage to the next, you have to ensure you've
backfilled. By backfilling, I mean you have developed the skills in other people around you who
are now supposed to be doing the work you once
did. They need to gain the skills to do the job as
well as you can (or could) — and maybe even better than you can (or ever could). Many of them
might, for the first time, be faced with having to
learn the full scope of their position responsibilities. Many might finally have to do the work and
tasks they're being paid to do — because you're
not doing their work for them any longer! As
a Stage 2 Leader, you need to delegate and trust
that others can do more than they currently are.
By having others do the work they can (or should)
be doing, you no longer are needed to be there all
the time, involved with every issue, or resolving

every problem. Wouldn't that be fun? As a participant in a leadership training program once said to me, "Delegation is where it's at!" I love that slogan. And when those words become not just a slogan, but a way of behaving that ensures others are given the challenge and opportunity to do the work they're supposed to be doing, you'll start positioning yourself more comfortably as a Stage 2 Leader.

Even though it's easy to say, "You need to delegate," believe me, I know letting go is hard. Years ago I was given the nickname "The Checklist Queen" by a colleague. At the time, I was volunteering as a professional organization's Professional Development Chair (and as such, was responsible for coordinating the logistics for 10 monthly educational programs). Now those of you who have planned events know this isn't all that difficult. However, there are numerous details to address before, during, and after each event to ensure there are no last minute snafus. Since there were few prior systems in place to guide my efforts, and being the systems-oriented person I am, I created a checklist of what I anticipated would need to be addressed to support each program. Then as each event occurred over the first few months, I tweaked the list to ensure it included every critical step (as well as several "nice-to-do" steps) so I wouldn't forget things, and so my successor could handle the job just as I had. Sounds great right? Well I thought so too! But shortly after I had trained and turned the reins over to my successor, I realized she wasn't following the checklist! She'd contact me just days before the upcoming event to ask a question on a task that should have been handled weeks before! She would also ask the "wrong" people the "wrong" questions at the "wrong" time! Invariably, I'd say to her or mutter to myself:

"Did you read the checklist?"

"According to the checklist, that should have been done weeks ago!"

"Why doesn't she just read the dang checklist?"

After venting to a colleague, he laughed and said, "What's wrong Checklist Queen? Isn't she following YOUR list?" Wow. He'd caught me. I was a bit too attached to my list and my way of co-ordinating the programs. Any deviations my successor made were "wrong" in my book. In reality, she'd not done anything wrong; she was getting the same great results. She was just going about it a bit differently than I had. Granted, her way didn't seem as organized as my way, but... (Let it go Liz. Just let it go).

Letting go is hard for many former exceptional doers. However, if you want to be a Stage 2 Leader, you need to ask yourself, "Why can't I let go? Is my successor not achieving the same results? If not,

I may need to stay engaged. If she is, what am I holding on to?"

Learn to trust others to have the right skills and abilities. Learn to delegate. Learn to verify results. Learn to support. Learn to let go.

"Giving people self-confidence is by far the most important thing that I can do. Because then they will act."
—Jack Welch

It's Your Team. Manage Them.

Another challenge in becoming a Stage 2 Leader for many managers is learning how to hold others accountable to do their jobs. I see several types of manager struggle with this: those who are new and now supervising former peers, those who succeed an extremely lax manager, and those who prefer to avoid conflict. If you struggle with holding your team accountable, keep in mind: Regardless of how you came to be their manager, your team is your team, so it's your responsibility to be the manager.

> **Holding your team accountable to do the jobs they're being paid to do is not being mean; it's being a manager, and that's your job.**

My company worked with a client's management team to develop stronger management skills throughout the organization. Being a large state agency, naturally some managers have had years on the job, while others are relatively new to their positions. As is typical, we're making headway a bit quicker with the individuals who are newer to

They need to do their jobs; you need to do yours. When that happens, you're better able to keep the entire team moving forward.

the management arena since they don't have to unlearn old habits in order to learn the new ones.

The most common problem we see with many of the managers is their hesitation to hold themselves and their team members accountable to do their respective jobs. The new or less confident managers fear the potential pushback from their former peers if they are now asked to perform the full scope of their job responsibilities.

Karen, a new manager shared her frustrations with me. She had inherited her team from her former manager, Josh. He was a nice man — but he was an ineffective manager. Josh, like many ineffective Stage 2 managers, thought being "nice" meant not holding team members accountable to do their jobs, so he didn't. Josh actually thought it was more efficient if he simply did many of their tasks himself since he could do them just as quickly. And by doing the work himself, he could also avoid the employees' questions and complaints. Shortly after her promotion, Karen started to challenge the team members to take ownership of their jobs. She was creating expectations where there had been few before. As a result, Karen had inherited a team which viewed her as a dictator on a power trip. Needless to say, her first several months in her new position were difficult. However, after Karen and I spoke briefly about Stage 2 Leadership, she realized that not only had her job changed, but so had her responsibilities. She needed to have a conversation with her staff to clarify that fact and communicate both her changed role and theirs.

A year later, Karen shared with me that her team had "turned the corner." After she'd clarified everyone's role, responsibilities, and their shared mission, things started to change. Her team members were working together more efficiently, and they were starting to respect her and her management skills. Karen had replaced a few employees and had guided several system reorganizations. Her team had achieved a few solid successes in her first year as a manager. By continuing to do her job as a Stage 2 Leader, Karen was confident they'd achieve many more in the years ahead.

When managers are planning to have a conversation with a team member who is not performing well, I suggest they not use the term "Difficult Conversation." This term, made popular by a book written in 2000 by Douglas Stone, Bruce Patton, and Sheila Heen, causes managers to envision potential conflicts, tears and other emotional interactions. As a result, managers often postpone the conversation or tell themselves things aren't so bad, so the conversations don't occur — and the poor behavior continues. Therefore, I suggest calling them Necessary

"Difficult Conversations" are really Necessary Conversations.[TM]

Conversations™ instead, which eliminates the excuses for not having these conversations. This simple terminology change helps managers view them as conversations that need to occur — not as potential arguments and drama to avoid.

I've been amazed at the number of clients who have said this simple tip has caused them to start having Necessary Conversations™ right away. Instead of walking past an employee and telling herself, "I need to talk to him about his attitude sometime" and then avoiding it, the manager will tell me, "I catch myself thinking: 'I need to talk to him about his attitude sometime,' but then I only take another step or two and say to myself, 'Wait. This is a Necessary Conversation™ we need to have now to resolve this and move on.'" The conversation then occurs right when the unacceptable behavior is observed. The conversation occurs in real-time and is much more objective. The emotions have not flared. The behavior is addressed. The issue is resolved. The manager has done her job, and all it took was a Necessary Conversation™.

Do you want to learn more about Necessary Conversations™?
If you'd like to learn more about how to hold Necessary Conversations™ to enhance your relationships with team members and improve their performance, see Section 3. Consider investing in a 5-Stages Workbook, Training Kit, or bring Liz or one of her team members into your organization for on-site training!

When you've backfilled effectively by coaching, delegating, training, and holding people accountable to do the jobs they're being paid to do, the doers who are now doing the work often are now solving their own problems.

When this occurs, it's an indication that you have effectively trained them to identify and resolve issues as they arise instead of simply dumping them on your desk. More importantly, it's an indication that you have identified that your time is better spent on managing and not on doing the work or solving the problems of your team members. **They need to do their jobs; you need to do yours. When that happens, you're better able to keep the entire team moving forward. And when that happens, you're a Stage 2 Leader.**

>> Whether your transition into your new position was smooth or it was clumsy, the net result is: You're the manager.

So take the time to talk with your team. It's your responsibility to hold them accountable.

- Clarify what your role is and what theirs are.
- Discuss what your responsibilities are and what theirs are.
- Discuss what your organization or department's mission is and what it is you all are supposed to do as a team to fulfill the mission.
- Clarify your team's priorities and what metrics and methods you'll be using to gauge everyone's performance and the team's progress.
- Be open. Be honest. Be fair. The systems previously developed are useful, objective tools to guide you and your entire team in doing the work that needs to be done. Use them. Leverage them. Refine them as needed. They provided value for you in Stage 1; they're even more valuable in Stage 2.

Be an Effective Stage 2 Leader:
Do Your Job, Not Theirs

When you successfully operate as a Stage 2 Leader, your actions free you to focus on the work you're supposed to be doing as a manager: managing a team of effective doers who are using the systems, policies, and procedures to do their jobs.

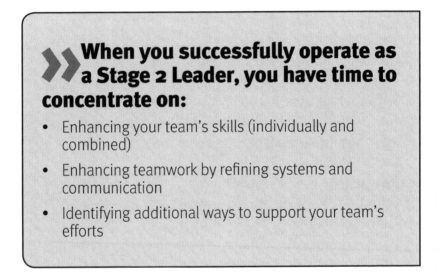

>> When you successfully operate as a Stage 2 Leader, you have time to concentrate on:

- Enhancing your team's skills (individually and combined)

- Enhancing teamwork by refining systems and communication

- Identifying additional ways to support your team's efforts

Basically, you are helping your team by clearing real and potential road blocks for them and ensuring they have the resources they need, when they need them, to do their jobs. To move solidly and effectively into a Stage 2 Leadership mindset, you

"The best executive is the one who has sense enough to pick good men to do what he wants done, and self-restraint enough to keep from meddling with them while they do it."
—Theodore Roosevelt

have to develop others by delegating, training, and supporting them to do their work. In other words, you help them understand and fully utilize the systems and tools available to them to do their jobs, so you can manage. **Let me put it another way: you have to do your job so they can do theirs. When that happens, you move from being a good manager to a great manager. Good managers are expected; great managers are respected.**

It's "Office Work," Not Busy Work

In addition to developing the ability to hold yourself and your team members accountable, the shift to Stage 2 poses an additional struggle for many new managers. It's difficult for many newer managers to understand the value of the "office work" now required of them. It's a tough psychological shift to accept that things such as monitoring systems, tracking reports for trends and deviations, and addressing personnel issues can be as valuable and rewarding as personally making 487 widgets or closing a big sale.

However, to make a solid shift to Stage 2 Leadership, new managers need to understand there is tremendous value in what effective managers do, even if it's not as tangible. One of my clients promoted Keith, the star sales representative, to manage the construction company's sales team. However, Keith was struggling with his new

Good managers are expected...

management role. He knew the position would provide him with future growth opportunities within the company, but from his perspective, the "bureaucracy" of having to generate and review reports, sit in meetings, and deal with personnel issues was a waste of time. At one point Keith said to me, "I wish I could just focus on real work again." His idea of "real work" meant hands-on sales. However, now he was "stuck in an office" even though he tried to help with sales as much as possible. His was a classic case of a manager who had not yet made the mental shift to Stage 2 Leadership. He didn't understand how his job as a Stage 2 Leader could really help his team.

After I discussed Stage 2 Leadership with him, Keith understood the need for an individual to mentally as well as physically shift behaviors as leadership roles changed. His job was no longer about doing the work himself. It was about getting the work done through his team's coordinated efforts. As a manager, his job was to coordinate and support his team members' efforts as he cleared roadblocks for them.

great *managers are respected.*

Now, because of his role change, Keith had to make a decision: did he want to be a manager and manage the sales team or return to Stage 1 Leadership and sales? Where would he find the most personal, long-term satisfaction? Where would he be of most value to his team and to the organization?

After a few days of thinking and self-reflection, Keith decided to stay and grow into his management role. He believed he could best help his team as their manager — as he understood them and their needs better than anyone. Keith realized he would best serve his team by shifting his mindset and actions to become an effective Stage 2 Leader. He'd focus on guiding, supporting, and leveraging the skills and talents of his team to generate even greater sales. He'd focus on managing and supporting his team instead of trying to sell along with his team. He'd support them. He'd manage. He'd become a Stage 2 Leader. And he did.

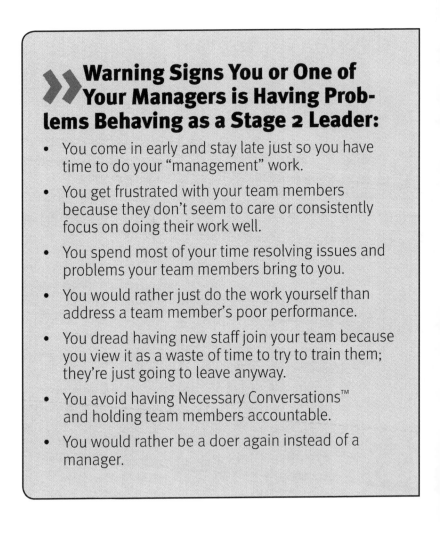

>> Warning Signs You or One of Your Managers is Having Problems Behaving as a Stage 2 Leader:

- You come in early and stay late just so you have time to do your "management" work.

- You get frustrated with your team members because they don't seem to care or consistently focus on doing their work well.

- You spend most of your time resolving issues and problems your team members bring to you.

- You would rather just do the work yourself than address a team member's poor performance.

- You dread having new staff join your team because you view it as a waste of time to try to train them; they're just going to leave anyway.

- You avoid having Necessary Conversations™ and holding team members accountable.

- You would rather be a doer again instead of a manager.

The two biggest challenges most Stage 2 Leaders face is learning to delegate and holding team members accountable to do their jobs. However, until you or your managers who are struggling with Stage 2 Leadership accept that you are spending your time doing work your team members are currently being paid to do, you and your team can not move forward. You will continue to operate in the 'Doing' and 'Developing Systems' space, thereby prohibiting your team members from learning how and taking on their full position responsibilities. Why should they? You do it. Until you stop doing the work they were hired and are being paid to do and start doing the work you are now being paid to do, you have no right to be frustrated with your team. They're doing exactly what you are training and allowing them to do. Stop doing their work. Stop providing all the answers and solving the problems they bring to you. Let go and teach them how to do their work. Teach them how to think through problems that arise in the course of their work. Help them learn how to analyze and resolve issues. Help them gain new skills and enhance their own marketability. Hold them accountable to do the work they are being paid to do. That's what Stage 2 Leaders do.

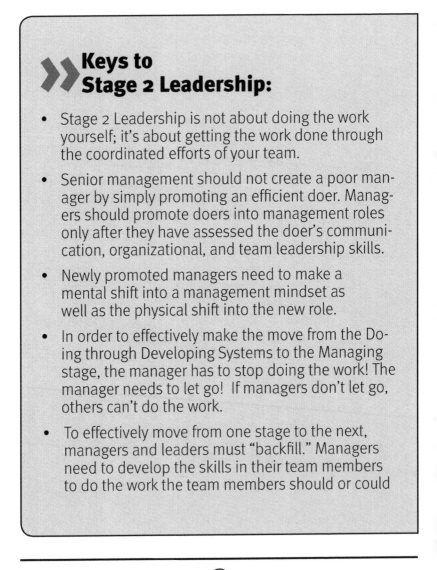

Keys to Stage 2 Leadership:

- Stage 2 Leadership is not about doing the work yourself; it's about getting the work done through the coordinated efforts of your team.

- Senior management should not create a poor manager by simply promoting an efficient doer. Managers should promote doers into management roles only after they have assessed the doer's communication, organizational, and team leadership skills.

- Newly promoted managers need to make a mental shift into a management mindset as well as the physical shift into the new role.

- In order to effectively make the move from the Doing through Developing Systems to the Managing stage, the manager has to stop doing the work! The manager needs to let go! If managers don't let go, others can't do the work.

- To effectively move from one stage to the next, managers and leaders must "backfill." Managers need to develop the skills in their team members to do the work the team members should or could

do. Once that happens, the leader is able to stop doing the work him or herself and can move to the next stage.

- Stage 2 Leaders need to hold themselves and their teams accountable to do the jobs they're being paid to do. Regardless of how they came to be the manager or what their predecessors have or have not done, the teams are now their teams to manage.

- "Difficult Conversations" are really Necessary Conversations™.

- Managers who manage effectively spend the bulk of their core work hours managing and NOT doing the work the team members should or could be doing, resolving problems for them, and otherwise doing, fixing, and expediting staff work. The manager manages; the doers do.

- Effective Stage 2 Leaders understand the value in what managers do, even if it's not as tangible or as easily quantified as the front-line, hands-on doers' work.

STAGE 3

Transition from Managing to Leading

Why are you always playing catch-up just to keep up? What's it all for?

THE NEAR-SIGHTED EFFECT:
Spotting Trouble in the Transition to Stage 3 Leadership

When managers fail to transition to a Stage 3 Leadership mindset, they tend to be so busy being busy they don't have time to think or plan effectively. They tend to be more reactive than proactive.

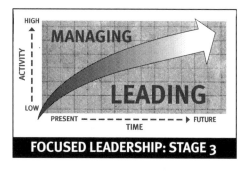

FOCUSED LEADERSHIP: STAGE 3

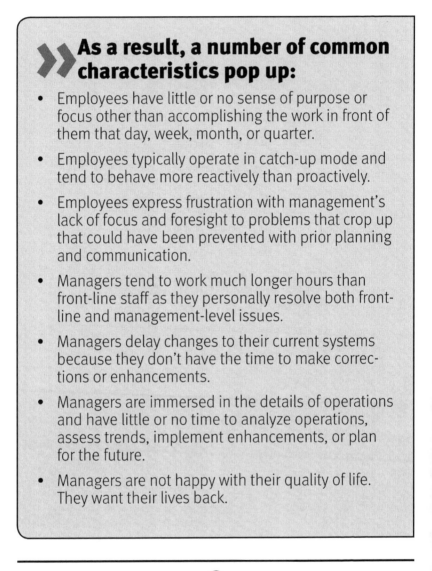

>> As a result, a number of common characteristics pop up:

- Employees have little or no sense of purpose or focus other than accomplishing the work in front of them that day, week, month, or quarter.

- Employees typically operate in catch-up mode and tend to behave more reactively than proactively.

- Employees express frustration with management's lack of focus and foresight to problems that crop up that could have been prevented with prior planning and communication.

- Managers tend to work much longer hours than front-line staff as they personally resolve both front-line and management-level issues.

- Managers delay changes to their current systems because they don't have the time to make corrections or enhancements.

- Managers are immersed in the details of operations and have little or no time to analyze operations, assess trends, implement enhancements, or plan for the future.

- Managers are not happy with their quality of life. They want their lives back.

Managing is Not The Same Thing As Leading

When I ask my clients what the difference is between managing and leading, I get variations of Warren G. Bennis's definition: "Managers do things right; leaders do the right things." That's wonderful — but when I ask them how, as leaders, would they know what the right things to do are, I'm met with their deer-in-the-headlights looks. They don't know. Most managers don't know, because they're managing, not leading.

>> **Because of this common confusion, I have my clients look at the difference in managers and leaders as basically this:**

Managers are responsible for the here and now (up to one year out), and leaders focus on what's coming next.

1. What do we as an organization, department, or entity need to have in place to ensure our relevance and competitiveness three, four, five, ten or more years from now?

2. Who do we want as our customers three, four, five, ten or more years from now?

3. What will our customers of the future need us to provide?

4. How will we position ourselves differently from our competition?

5. Putting all of the known and unknown operational, staffing, financial, and other challenges aside, what must we accomplish to ensure our future?

6. Given the above, what are the right things we leaders need to think about to ensure the organization's long-term success?

Leaders think strategically and identify answers to these types of questions. These questions and thoughts are easy to voice, but they're not at all easy to respond to when you're already working 50, 60, 70+ hours a week.

As busy managers, you're already trying to ensure all current resource commitments, staffing issues, equipment concerns, and budget restrictions are addressed. So when you hear there are more and larger challenges ahead, like most managers you probably think: "No more! Please no more!" Like most managers, you are probably already physically and mentally maxed out. You cannot effectively think strategically because your brain is already working in overdrive trying to stay on top of all of the management concerns you face each day. So when you're asked to think

"The person who knows 'how' will always have a job. The person who knows 'why' will always be his boss."
—Diane Ravitch

even bigger, more challenging, and less tangibly three, four, five, or more years into the future, you rightly think, "Yeah right. I've got real issues to deal with now. I don't have time to dream."

Make the Leap to Leadership

As an organization's leader, a fundamental leadership responsibility of yours is to ensure the organization will continue to fulfill its mission, provide a livelihood for your employees, and deliver products or services to your customers long after you leave. Once you internalize that responsibility, you begin to move into a Stage 3 Leadership mindset.

I had the opportunity to see one of my clients make the leap from being a manager to being a leader. I was preparing for our strategic planning session with his senior team, when Kevin, a 60-year-old serial entrepreneur, walked into the conference room and said, "Liz, I finally understand what my job is here." Now keep in mind, Kevin owns the company. He said, "My job is to create a future for this company. I need to build a strong management team to ensure this organization is still around after I'm long gone." That's it! He "got it!" Kevin finally understood, deep in his gut, what his job as the company's leader was. He needed to develop the management and leadership skills in his managers so they could continue to run the company when he retired. His company would no longer be dependent upon him alone. It would be dependent upon a team of solid leaders, managers, and doers. If his managers developed stronger management skills, he would have time to lead, plan for the organization's future, and do the right thing for his company. Kevin was finally thinking as a Stage 3 Leader. Now he needed to do his job as a Stage 3 Leader so his team could do theirs.

"The task of the leader is to get his people from where they are to where they have not been."
—Henry Kissinger

Be An Effective Stage 3 Leader: Free Up Mental Space to Lead

Dorothy, a senior manager, asked me what the difference was between a manager and a leader. I told her: *A manager is responsible for taking care of the here and now. A manager ensures that resources are used efficiently and plans how best to leverage staff, equipment, materials, and capital to fulfill the production requirements this week, this month, this quarter, and this year. A leader thinks: "In addition to our near-term production requirements, what's coming next? What type of organization do we need to be three, four, five, or more years from now to be successful?"* Given that definition, Dorothy sat back and said, "I'm definitely not a leader. I don't have time to think about the future. I'm overwhelmed trying to keep the here and now under control. How do I find the time to lead?"

Dorothy's situation is incredibly common.

Most managers are so busy being busy, they don't have time to think strategically. They don't have time to think as leaders. **However, if you want your organization to be viable in the future, you have to find the time to lead. You have to make the time. And surprisingly, as a leader, you already have the time — you're just not using your time correctly.**

As a manager, if you are swamped every day with a myriad of management tasks, you will not have the time, nor will you — as I say — have the "mental free space" to think strategically about the organization's future. So you won't. As a result, your team, your department, or (if you're the owner or the organization's leader) your organization will continuously be in catch-up mode — always scrambling to remain viable, never seeming to be able to get on top of, or ahead of, the curve. You react more than plan and act. You will be incredibly busy now, but your viability in the future becomes a big question mark.

Until you free up your time and some of your mental capacity to focus on "What's next?" it's terribly difficult to become an effective leader.

You see, you can't lead until you've taught others how to manage. Many managers try to both manage and lead, and as a result they end up being stressed out Stage 2 Leaders with limited effectiveness in planning for the future.

So how can Dorothy become a Stage 3 Leader? She needs to start holding her supervisors and managers accountable to do their jobs. They need to do their jobs more fully as team leaders, project managers, supervisors, and managers. They need to take ownership and responsibility for their own work and teams. For Dorothy, that means she needs to coach her supervisors and managers and then hold them accountable to do the tough things supervisors and managers have to do.

If you want your organization to be viable in the future, you have to find the time to lead.

"Management is efficiency in climbing the ladder of success; leadership determines whether the ladder is leaning against the right wall."
—Stephen R. Covey

>>Leaders coach their managers to:

- Develop their communications and interpersonal skills to improve their interactions with their team members

- Have the Necessary Conversations™ with their own team members who are not performing well

- Coach and hold their team members accountable to do their jobs

- Identify and proactively solve their teams' and their own problems

- Help their team members learn to identify and solve their own problems

- Deal directly with unhappy customers. (Don't push them up to the leader to address.)

- Determine and justify their own resource and staffing needs

- Guide their own hiring and termination actions

- Track their project and team goals with their teams to ensure they are supporting the department's mission

As a Stage 3 Leader, Dorothy needs to stop doing her supervisors' and managers' management tasks. Until her managers are held accountable to do their jobs and manage themselves and their teams effectively, Dorothy won't be able to lead. Until they develop solid Stage 2 Leadership skills, Dorothy will struggle to attain Stage 3 Leadership.

You can't lead until you've taught others how to manage.

Develop Your Stage 3 Leadership Skills: Backfill to Move On

As a struggling Stage 3 Leader like Dorothy, if you don't think strategically and push your team to ensure your organization's viability in the future, you run the risk of being overrun by the competition. Effective Stage 3 Leaders know this. So, just as good managers (and effective Stage 2 Leaders) know they have to develop staff around them to "backfill" to do the work, Stage 3 Leaders realize they too need to backfill and develop the management skills in others around them.

Stage 3 Leaders need to let go of select management tasks so others can learn to manage. And Stage 3 Leaders need to develop solid supervisory and management skills in as many of their managers and team members as possible. Good managers realize they need to delegate, train, support, and challenge staff to be able to take on select management tasks for their individual, team, and organizational growth and development.

By expanding the number of employees who can effectively employ basic to sophisticated management skills, a good manager builds teams of self-reliant problem solvers, capable of thinking critically, working collaboratively, managing projects, and addressing complex and challenging team issues. Very basically, this creates an environment within which the effective manager can go to meetings, conferences, or — yes — even go on vacation, and the organization runs just fine without the manager being there! Again, this is easy to say but not easy for many managers to do. It's that old control issue again.

Remember: If managers don't let go, others can't do the work.

Share Your Strategy for Success

Once a manager effectively shifts into the Stage 3 Leadership mode and develops management skills in others, the manager now has the capability and "mental free space" to lead. Stage 3 Leaders have purposely created the mental space and time needed to think strategically. For Stage 3 Leaders, strategic planning is a critical leadership tool. Focused, clear strategic plans are their road maps to their organizations' successful

*"If you can't explain it simply,
you don't understand it well enough."
—Albert Einstein*

future. To leverage their plans, effective Stage 3 Leaders ensure the strategic plan is communicated to and understood by all employees in the organization to ensure every employee — and I do mean every employee — understands the vision (i.e., the BIG goal of the organization). By sharing this with every employee, Stage 3 Leaders enhance their employees' sense of purpose. As a result, the employees are less likely to feel as if they're always playing catch-up just to keep up. They know what they're all working towards. They know what it's all for. Good strategic plans also provide insights into how each employee (through their individual work and various projects) can help achieve the organization's vision. Stage 3 Leaders create the focus, clarify the target, and share the plan.

"Get Outside" to Gain Insight

A key source of insight for the Stage 3 Leader to help in developing the strategic plan is to "get outside" the organization — physically and intellectually.

When this happens, the Stage 3 Leader can meet other leaders, study the external environment, politics, industry, and demographic changes that do and will affect the industry and business. A Stage 2 Leader doesn't typically have a lot of time outside the organization; a Stage 3 Leader doesn't succeed without "getting outside." Developing relationships, as well as learning and interacting with various customer industries, complementary and competitive business leaders, and governmental forces, allows the strategically thinking Stage 3 Leaders to gain broader insights into issues which currently do or might impact the organization or the industry in the future. Being "outside" the organization allows Stage 3 Leaders to consider various external factors when planning for their organization's future. Without these external perspectives and insights, it is easy for leaders to confine themselves to their current organizational limitations, restrictions, and viewpoints. However, when they learn about and can focus on the issues being faced by the competition, the industry, and the regulators, Stage 3 Leaders can ask: "Given what we have learned, what must we do next to ensure our future?" versus "What is difficult for us now?"

This "What do we need to do next" mindset enables Stage 3 Leaders to then plan and position their organizations for long-term survival — and for long-term success. It's another step toward ensuring they can get their lives back by staying ahead of the curve instead of clawing their way up the competitive curve.

Be the Leader They Need

Do you remember Dominic the CEO of the manufacturing company I introduced you to in the beginning of this book? Dominic said, "I want my life back. I love working, but I've got to stop working 50, 60, and 70 hour weeks. Something's got to change around here." Someone, not something, did need to change: Dominic. More specifically, Dominic's thinking needed to change. He needed to think and then lead differently. Dominic needed to become a Stage 3 Leader. In his current management mode, he was handcuffed to the business. Dominic was working incredibly long hours, dealing with issues his managers could and should have been handling, and positioning himself as the go-to guy for every major — and relatively minor — issue. He was burning out, his management team and employees were frustrated, and his company was suffering because of it.

As I shared with Dominic, if he started to do his job as a Stage 3 Leader, his managers would develop stronger skills in coaching and guiding the front-line employees. Then he and his management team could plan for the organization's future and communicate it to all of the employees. The employees would then know where the company was headed and how they fit in now and were going to fit in in the future. Dominic and his team would no longer play catch-up; they were going to play "Watch us move up!" That's what happens when doers do, managers manage, and leaders lead. Dominic understood. As his eyes lit up, he said, "Something's going to change around here...me!"

If any of these warning signs sound like

"The most dangerous leadership myth is that leaders are born — that there is a genetic factor to leadership. This myth asserts that people simply either have certain charismatic qualities or not. That's nonsense; in fact, the opposite is true. Leaders are made rather than born."
—Warren G. Bennis

❯❯ Warning Signs You or One of Your Managers is Having Problems Behaving as a Stage 3 Leader:

- You focus on what's expected of you to produce or deliver over the next few weeks or year but fail to anticipate what you need to do beyond that to stay viable and relevant.

- You are waiting for things to slow down and 'get back to normal' so you will have time to plan.

- You don't dedicate time to get outside your organization — either by physically attending educational events or by simply reading and observing what's happening with other organizations — to identify ways to strategically enhance your organization.

- You don't develop basic problem solving and management skills in others so you have the physical time and mental 'free space' to think strategically.

you, it's time to realize you need to slow down in order for you, your team, and your organization to speed up and stay viable and relevant. Until you stop allowing yourself to use the excuse of being too busy to plan, you won't be able to stop the frantic pace and feel of your organization. Don't think your team believes your excuses of having no time to plan. They know, if you had a plan, things wouldn't be so frantic. Stage 3 Leaders think, plan and act strategically. They anticipate busy and slack cycles. They plan for them. They prepare their teams for them. And they lead their teams through them. That's what Stage 3 Leaders do.

"Don't think your team believes your excuses of having no time to plan. They know, if you had a plan, things wouldn't be so frantic."

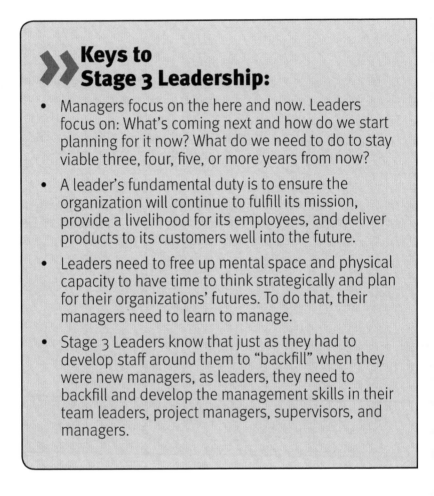

>> Keys to
>> Stage 3 Leadership:

- Managers focus on the here and now. Leaders focus on: What's coming next and how do we start planning for it now? What do we need to do to stay viable three, four, five, or more years from now?

- A leader's fundamental duty is to ensure the organization will continue to fulfill its mission, provide a livelihood for its employees, and deliver products to its customers well into the future.

- Leaders need to free up mental space and physical capacity to have time to think strategically and plan for their organizations' futures. To do that, their managers need to learn to manage.

- Stage 3 Leaders know that just as they had to develop staff around them to "backfill" when they were new managers, as leaders, they need to backfill and develop the management skills in their team leaders, project managers, supervisors, and managers.

- Stage 3 Leaders understand the importance of focused, clear strategic planning to provide the clarity and focus they and their teams need.

- Stage 3 Leaders "get outside" the organization — physically and intellectually — to learn from and meet other leaders and to study the external environment, politics, industry, and demographic changes that do and will affect their industry and their organizations.

- When Stage 3 Leaders lead, managers manage, and doers do.

When leaders lead,

managers manage,

and doers do,

everyone knows what

they're all working toward.

Who's going to be leading your company in the future?

Are they ready?

STAGE 4

Transition from Leading to Mentoring

Are your employees capable of supporting, managing, and leading your future organization?

THE KNOWLEDGE-GAP EFFECT:
Spotting Trouble in the Transition to Stage 4 Leadership

When an organization's leader fails to make the transition to a Stage 4 Leader's mindset and behaviors, more emphasis will be placed on physical and technological infrastructure enhancements for the future than on the team's intellectual development needs. The employees' skill sets and knowledge become strained, overwhelmed, and potentially obsolete. By not providing the team with the training and skills

FOCUSED LEADERSHIP: STAGE 4

they need to do their jobs efficiently now and in the future, the non-transitioning Stage 3 Leader is causing the organization to start to shift out of balance.

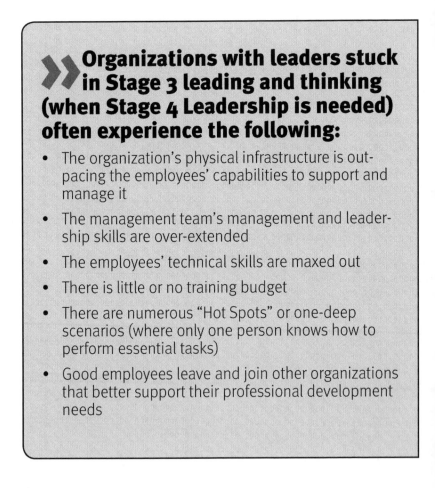

>> Organizations with leaders stuck in Stage 3 leading and thinking (when Stage 4 Leadership is needed) often experience the following:

- The organization's physical infrastructure is out-pacing the employees' capabilities to support and manage it

- The management team's management and leader-ship skills are over-extended

- The employees' technical skills are maxed out

- There is little or no training budget

- There are numerous "Hot Spots" or one-deep scenarios (where only one person knows how to perform essential tasks)

- Good employees leave and join other organizations that better support their professional development needs

If your actions inspire others to dream more, learn more, do more, and become more, you are a leader.
—John Quincy Adams

When these scenarios happen, the customers are negatively impacted. From the customers' perspective, they see an organization that used to serve them well now behaving as if it's too big to care about them and service them effectively any more. The personal touch, dedicated customer focus, and care customers are used to receiving start to wane. As a result, the customers begin to look for alternative providers. The company with the focused, bright future starts to lose its customers of the future. An effective Stage 4 Leader realizes the need to balance the physical infrastructure development with the intellectual infrastructure development to ensure the organization's future becomes a reality.

Be an Effective Stage 4 Leader: Boost Your Intellectual Infrastructure

So how do you become a Stage 4 Leader? When you've got your organization pointed and moving in the right direction for its future (i.e., you have a clear strategic plan in place), it's time to think about Stage 4 Leadership. After clarifying what type of entity the organization needs to become in Stage 3 via the strategic plan, a Stage 4 Leader not only sees the future, but also understands his or her "evolved" organization will need new and different skill sets — and possibly different staff positions — to support, manage, and lead the organization as it will be in the future. However, many of the needed future skill sets and positions are currently underdeveloped or nonexistent within the current employee population.

>> Therefore, as a Stage 4 Leader, you will need to backfill even more than during Stages 1–3.

As a Stage 4 Leader, you will focus your energies to ensure your organization's human intellectual infrastructure is being developed, along with your organization's physical infrastructure, so the entire team has the ability to support the potentially larger, more sophisticated organization of the future.

Now all of that seems fairly logical. But why is it so important that a Stage 4 Leader develop an intense focus on developing skills and enhancing knowledge? As Susan Meisinger, the former president and CEO of the Society for Human Resources Management, said, "The one thing competitors can't quickly access is the brains of your work force."

Your competitors today and tomorrow may well be able to ramp up their physical infrastructures, virtual capabilities, and other hard resources to compete; however, developing a talented and knowledgeable work force takes time.

I am also a firm believer that it's the leadership team's job to ensure their employees continue to be marketable with strong skills. I know that may seem odd to many, but my most successful clients with the most engaged employees are those that are continually challenging their employees to learn, develop new skills, and take on new responsibilities. The organization is benefiting from the innovation and energy of the employees, and the employees continually add new, marketable skills to leverage if and when they decide to work someplace else. Win-win. With that in mind, it's time to ramp-up the brainpower.

To drive this intellectual infrastructure development, you need to focus on staff development, training, cross-training, coaching, mentoring, strategic hiring, and planning for succession throughout the organization. Leadership succession and overall position succession planning become a prime concern for you now. As a Stage 4 Leader, you need to accept that if you do not enhance knowledge and build skills deep within the organization, or acquire them externally, your organization will not be able to survive in its future state. Your team's workforce and leadership team will be inadequate, underdeveloped, or simply outdated.

"The conventional definition of management is getting work done through people, but real management is developing people through work."
—Agha Hasan Abedi

Avoid Inadequacy!
You will need to ramp up your employees' skill sets and staffing infrastructure to support the future organization. Do this while the organization increases its physical infrastructure, facilities,

Effective Stage 4 Leadership will create effective Stage 2 and Stage 3 Leaders.

software systems, technologies, and equipment to support the future organization.

One of my professional services clients experienced what happens when an organization's leader doesn't move into Stage 4 Leadership when the company needs a Stage 4 Leader. Julie, the company's owner, had moved rather easily into Stage 3 Leadership. She had transitioned her thinking and her leadership behaviors from managing to leading. As a result, she had developed a team of managers around her who were taking hold of their Stage 2 and Stage 3 Leadership responsibilities. The management team had expanded operations, added new staff, and realized rapid success. However, after roughly three years of growth, employee and management turnover rates were trending dramatically upward. Customer satisfaction was trending downward, and so was employee morale. Many of the leadership team's successes were teetering on instability. The strong company of the future was starting to look more like an unreachable dream.

Because of the growth in operations and the increase in complexity of their operational issues, the management team and many of the employees had reached the limits of their intellectual know-how. **They didn't have the experience, training, or skills to continue to effectively run the organization they had become, much less**

the organization they were working to become in the future. While Julie had led the charge to enhance the company's physical infrastructure to house and logistically support a larger, more sophisticated organization, she hadn't focused on enhancing the organization's intellectual infrastructure as well. While Julie and the leadership team had built a physically larger business, it had not focused on supporting the employees' changing needs. **The management team and employees needed additional skills, insights, support, and enhanced resources to operate and lead the company as it was and would be in the future. The managers and employees were overwhelmed with the growing complexity of the work.** They were making frequent operational and managerial mistakes. Their underdeveloped skills were becoming increasingly apparent to them — and to their customers. The once strong company and team strained to meet current demands. Customers were complaining. Customers were leaving. Their solid business infrastructure was starting to crack. They needed Julie to be a Stage 4 Leader and focus on developing or bringing in the needed intellect and skills.

A manufacturing company — led by its founder, Jon — is another example of a client I've worked with to enhance both his and his team's strategic planning practices, management, and leadership

"I start with the premise that the function of leadership is to produce more leaders, not more followers."
—Ralph Nader

skills. Jon is an incredibly smart, self-taught man who is constantly focusing on where his company needs to be five, 10, and 15 years into the future. Over the years, Jon's also become extremely knowledgeable in not only cost-effective, efficient manufacturing, but also in efficient business management practices. An amazing characteristic of this company is there are only a handful of employees who have advanced degrees. Most of the employees only have high school educations. In spite of this, the company is more leading edge, efficient, and organized than many of its competitors and global clients. Why? Jon has constantly pushed systems development, self-improvement, team and leadership development, employee cross-training, customer relationship building, problem solving, etc. If you are not willing to constantly learn, grow, and be challenged to think about the work you do, this is not the company for you. As a result of Jon's focus on developing intellectual skills throughout the organization, his core management team members think as Stage 3 Leaders do. They regularly ask, "What do we need to do next and how can we keep current operations running smoothly as we transition to newer technologies?" Jon's Stage 4 Leadership has created a pool of effective Stage 2 and 3 Leaders.

Develop Deep Talent Pools

In Stage 4 Leadership, developing talent needs to happen organization-wide, not just within select departments or with a few select employees. Stage 4 Leaders naturally focus on ensuring there are potential leadership successors being groomed. However, Stage 4 Leaders also ensure that successors are being developed or that cross-training is occurring for every position within the organization. (Yes, I do mean for every position within the organization.) Very few organizations these days can afford to have excess staff positions. Every position is important. Therefore, every position should have the systems in place (See Stage 1 Leadership) to ensure that if its primary "doer" is out, leaves, or is otherwise unable to do the job, that position's work continues to flow.

When you as a Stage 4 Leader orchestrate the development of skills with all employees, by default, pools of talent are created deep and wide throughout the entire organization.

The workforce becomes smarter and more agile. By identifying talent and continuously developing skills with all employees throughout the organization (management to front-line), you

"Hot spots" are those one-deep scenarios: Positions within an organization where only one person knows how to perform essential tasks.

demonstrate to all staff that every employee is important. Every position is important. In fact, every position is critical. Therefore, every employee needs to know what skills are needed now and what skills will be needed in the organization in the future. As a result, every employee can better understand how he or she fits in now and how he or she needs to grow and develop to fit into the organization in the future.

Another benefit of an organization-wide emphasis on skills development is the creation of a culture of learning. The employees develop a sense of camaraderie. Everyone is learning something new; skills development or skills training is not just for those who "need to improve." Organization-wide learning and skills enhancement become "just the way things are around here" and training no longer is viewed as punitive. It's viewed correctly: an opportunity to gain new insights, skills and techniques to enable all team members to do their jobs more effectively now and in the future.

Distinguish and Extinguish Hot Spots

A Stage 4 Leadership mindset and its related behaviors also have the benefit of helping to uncover hidden "Hot Spots" within an organization. I alluded to them earlier, but hot spots are those one-deep scenarios: positions within an organization

Training: an opportunity to gain new insights, skills, and techniques to enable all team members to do their jobs more effectively now and into the future.

where only one person (or an unacceptably low number of staff) knows how to perform essential tasks. An essential task may well be a task the highest paid person typically handles, or it could be a task performed by one of the clerks in the shipping department. Whatever the task is, it's critical to the organization because when the current person who performs the task is out, no one else knows what to do! Workflow stops. That's critical. That's a hot spot.

By identifying organizational hot spots, you can quickly identify where cross-training needs to occur or, at a bare minimum, processes need to be documented.

A few years ago, I worked with a hospital system to kick off their leadership-succession planning program. As we worked through an initial "hit by a bus" exercise (i.e., If you were hit by a bus after work today, identify two or three individuals who could immediately step in and keep things going in your area until you returned or a replacement was found), we started to notice an interesting trend. Monica, a senior staff member's name, kept appearing as a first choice to fill in for numerous positions. However, few of the other staff members had that same capability. When we started to analyze the skills that enabled Monica to have such broad appeal, it became apparent her training and prior job experiences provided her with unique insights others didn't have. This understanding allowed the planning team to then identify additional training, cross-training, and job shadowing programs which, when implemented, would help develop broader skills in other employees as well.

Don't use a mirror to determine the needed skills of the future; use the vision.

Don't Try to Create Clones

A potential danger awaiting you as you move into Stage 4 is the desire to create clones of yourself. It's an easy mistake to make. Why wouldn't you want to? Your skills, insights, and abilities all contributed to the organization's success so far, right? Yes. However, the skills that were needed to get the company to where it is today may not be the same skills the company will need in its management and leadership team going forward. Keep the organization's strategic vision in mind. What type of organization are you creating? What skills and talent will the company need to succeed? Don't use a mirror to determine the needed skills of the future; use the vision.

Drive Skill Development

Even though much of the coordination for employee training and development is managed by the Human Resources (HR) department, an effective Stage 4 Leader holds all managers, not just HR, responsible for supporting and developing employee skills. The direct-report managers know — or should know — better than HR what their staff members know or do not know. The direct-report managers know — or should know — better than HR what skills and positions their department will need to effectively support the organization as it will be in the future. Therefore, all managers need to be key players in the process of developing the organization's intellectual infrastructure. HR needs to be their guide, mentor, and facilitator in documenting missing skills, clarifying competencies and training terminology, as well as sourcing and coordinating the needed training. **HR is the guide, but the managers are the force behind the skills development.**

HR is the guide, but managers are the force behind the skills development.

Develop a Mentoring Mindset

Stage 4 is also a prime time for leaders to double back and assess the effectiveness of their

organization. Stage 4 Leaders assess the processes, procedures, training programs, and other
systems developed by Stage 1 Leaders to support
and develop staff throughout the organization.
Once assessed, Stage 4 Leaders can then direct
initiatives to strengthen any of these programs,
as well as to fill any gaps with less structured but
more relationship-oriented mentoring.

**A primary characteristic of Stage 4 Leaders
is a passion to develop a mentoring and
knowledge-sharing mindset throughout the
organization.**

A knowledge-sharing mindset ensures that at
the core of the organization's mentoring program,
sharing knowledge among staff members —
to develop skills and awareness in employees
throughout the organization — becomes a way of
life. Stage 4 Leaders recognize and communicate
throughout the organization that knowledge-
sharing can take the form of longer term, veteran
employees sharing historical information with
newer or younger staff, or it may as easily take
the form of tech-savvy staff sharing technology
tips and techniques with other staff to enhance
their productivity and efficiency. **The "how" of
sharing knowledge can take any direction or**

shape. Stage 4 Leaders keep focused on the objective: to develop skills and enhance team knowledge organization-wide.

One of my government clients is a unique, forward-thinking organization. They have been working diligently on internal staff development training and succession planning for over four years. However, there are several veteran staff members moving ever closer to retirement who still carry vast amounts of knowledge in their minds that doesn't neatly fit into any category of procedural documentation or staff development training. To continue the knowledge-sharing among staff and across departments, this client's leadership is encouraging dedicated mentoring conversations between longer-term and newer staff. These lunchtime discussions are unstructured, "why things are the way they are" conversations to help newer staff understand some of the current policies, regulations, procedural requirements, production flows, as well as interpersonal nuances of the organization. From this organization's Stage 4 Leader's perspective, Knowledge is Power. The more we can share, the better off our organization is and will be in the long run. I couldn't agree more.

Knowledge is power.

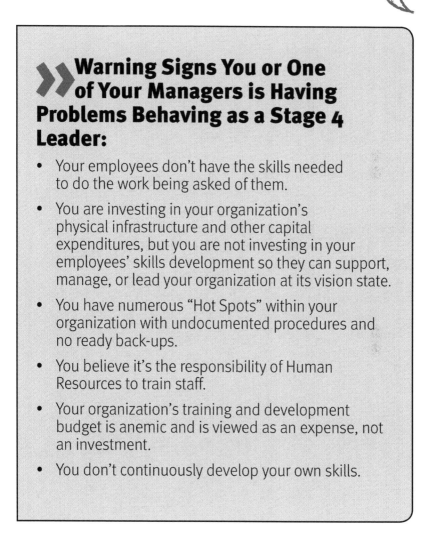

▶▶ Warning Signs You or One of Your Managers is Having Problems Behaving as a Stage 4 Leader:

- Your employees don't have the skills needed to do the work being asked of them.

- You are investing in your organization's physical infrastructure and other capital expenditures, but you are not investing in your employees' skills development so they can support, manage, or lead your organization at its vision state.

- You have numerous "Hot Spots" within your organization with undocumented procedures and no ready back-ups.

- You believe it's the responsibility of Human Resources to train staff.

- Your organization's training and development budget is anemic and is viewed as an expense, not an investment.

- You don't continuously develop your own skills.

If you have experienced any of these scenarios, you need to pull your leadership team together. It's time to change the way you have viewed training and developing your employees. You have probably been stuck viewing training as an expense instead of a strategic investment. If you don't invest in what is probably your most expensive business asset (i.e., your workforce), how can you expect it to continue to perform at peak levels going forward? Stage 4 Leaders understand the value of investing in their employees. Stage 4 Leaders understand the value of investing in all employees. Stage 4 Leaders understand the strategic importance of developing talent deep and wide within their organization. That's how they create value, stay relevant, and create an incredibly engaged and effective workforce. That's what Stage 4 Leaders do.

Invest in your most valuable asset.

>> Keys to Stage 4 Leadership:

- Stage 4 Leaders realize the "evolved" organization will need new and different skill sets, and possibly different staffing positions, to manage and lead the organization as it will be in the future.

- Stage 4 Leaders ensure their staffs have access to training, project and work challenges, and various mentoring opportunities to gain the skills needed to support the organization as it continues to evolve and grow.

- Savvy Stage 4 Leaders continuously assess staff knowledge, depth, and information needs across the organization to uncover hot spots or one-deep scenarios.

- Hot spots pinpoint opportunities for increased cross-training, documentation, and training aid development.

- Mentoring is a formal process, though it is often conducted informally. Mentoring is, at its core, sharing knowledge — older to younger, younger to older, skilled to less skilled.

Are you planning for
seamless transitions?

STAGE 5
Transition from Mentoring to Moving On

In this stage, you turn control of the organization you created or led over to those you have hired, trained, challenged, and mentored.

> ### THE ME-NOT-WE EFFECT:
> #### Spotting Trouble in the Transition To and Through Stage 5 Leadership

This final stage can take many forms. It can simply be handing off a responsibility to someone else (i.e., Stage 2 Leadership), or moving to another position within the organization, or it may present itself as you "Moving On" by leaving the organization altogether. The key idea is that whichever direction or form this "Moving On" mindset and behavior takes, whoever is taking over this responsibility for you

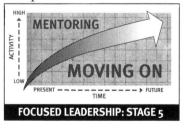

FOCUSED LEADERSHIP: STAGE 5

has been well-informed, trained, and coached and has the support systems in place to succeed.

In a traditional hierarchy, if it's your time to move on, you can only do so confidently when there's a team of skilled staff and managers capable of managing and leading the organization into its future. When that is in place, you are able to turn your attention even more towards outside endeavors. You may look to serve on outside boards to share your insights and perspectives, gain information on other industries, and further enhance your professional networks. When you decide to move on and leave your current position or the organization altogether, your "Moving On" endeavors may take the form of starting a new division or organization, transforming another organization, consulting, philanthrophy, or volunteering more. Or your "Moving On" may transition you to a quiet retirement.

"Moving on can simply be handing off a responsibility to someone else, or moving to another position within the organization, or it may present itself as you "Moving On" by leaving the organization altogether."

>> Stage 4 Leaders who have not planned for a focused transition to and through Stage 5 Leadership typically:

- Fail to listen to and respond to their internal need to stay with the organization a bit longer. Therefore, they leave only to end up coming back.

- Fail to listen to and respond to their need to move on, only to "retire" on the job.

- Fail to identify new opportunities outside the organization to put their incredible leadership and organizational development skills to work with other organizations who need their skill sets.

- Fail to provide opportunities to test or gauge the up-and-coming leaders' skills in leading the organization before stepping away.

- Fail to trust the new leaders' abilities to deal with the ups and downs and to succeed with the teams that had previously supported them.

- Fail to build and bridge professional relationships for their successors to ensure effective transitions of authority, responsibility, respect, and a desire for mutual success.

You Can Love It and Still Leave It

Stage 5 is most often a step many don't even realize is a focused leadership move. However, it's probably the most selfless move you as a leader can make. It's time to let go one last time.

A clear example of the move through Stage 5 Leadership is the transition of Bill Gates from leading Microsoft to creating and leading the Bill and Melinda Gates Foundation with his wife. He successfully developed one global organization with solid leaders. However, when he decided it was time for him to move on, he did. He transitioned himself and his skills to develop and lead another global organization — one with a philanthropic focus.

One of my financial services clients also demonstrated this last phase of focused leadership development by stepping away from an organization and employee population that loved and respected him. After taking on the CEO role, Rick, true to his nature, created a work environment conducive to strategic teamwork, open communication, and operational improvements. Efficiencies took off, morale rose, and applicants started to line up for the opportunity to work with this organization and become a part of this environment. Rick pushed the executive team and then the entire organization to focus on the future and then on knowledge management, comprehensive

Stage 5 is probably the most selfless move you as a leader can make. It's time to let go one last time.

114

staff development, and individual accountability. He made sure every manager and senior executive understood that staff development was a key responsibility for each of them. He also ensured there were pools of qualified candidates being developed throughout the organization for any open position. He would not allow only a select few star candidates to be identified and groomed; he wanted depth throughout the entire organization. He challenged his managers to enhance the employees' knowledge and skills at all levels of the organization. He was an incredible Stage 4 Leader.

Once the plans for continued development were defined, the physical infrastructure was evolving, and the necessary leadership development support and programs were in play, Rick decided to move on. He wanted to pursue another, more challenging professional role for himself. However, Rick left knowing he had backfilled sufficiently to ensure the future of the organization. There were successor Stage 2, 3, and 4 Leaders within the organization to guide it into the future. It was time for Rick to move on, and it was time for the new leaders to move up.

"Leaders don't create followers, they create more leaders."
—*Tom Peters*

》》Know When It's Time to Move On

Why does a Stage 5 Leader like Rick "Move On"? There are several possible reasons:

- His Stage 4 Leadership skills are no longer needed. Because of an effective Stage 4 Leader's skills, many of his Stage 4 Leadership characteristics are now echoed by others within the organization's leadership team. The developed leadership team regularly focuses on the future, the skills and knowledge needed, and the necessary physical infrastructure enhancements to assure their vision is achieved. Therefore, many of the veteran Stage 4 Leader's skills are no longer unique or fully utilized by the organization.

- He wants to pursue a new professional challenge, find a new "problem" to fix, or develop a new organization and team.

- He realizes his leadership skills may not be sufficient for the evolved organization. The organization may be outgrowing his skills and will soon have a need for different skills.

- He believes it is time for a leadership change to introduce "new blood and ideas."

Essentially, Stage 5 Leaders realize they no longer "fit" the organization now or as it will be. They know in their guts it's time for a change. They know it's time to move on.

Leadership is about what's right for the organization, not what feels right for the leader.

Moving On May Be the Hardest Phase

As Marshall Goldsmith notes in his book, *Succession: Are You Ready?*, many organizational leaders are surprised at how difficult, painful, and emotional the Moving On process can be. These leaders are now facing the very real prospect of other people calling the shots, other people determining the organization's strategy and focus, and other people now having the power, prestige, and respect they once had. That's a big change. In addition, the leader may well be leaving an organization she created or transformed into a success. Also the leader is moving from a known realm of responsibility into an unknown realm of new challenges. If facing retirement, the leader may have no known major challenges ahead. Going from "full-steam ahead!" to "does anyone care if I have any steam?" can be a somewhat confusing and depressing scenario. Because of this hesitation, I've seen several unsuccessful Stage 5 Leaders leave only to do a U-turn and come back to the organization at the first hint of management missteps, trouble, or customer dissatisfaction. They came back "to save" their organizations.

However, their professional U-turns have more to do with their individual boredom than with the current "crisis" confronting the company. The crisis was in their inability to plan for their job as a Stage 5 Leader as they had planned for Stages 1–4. Stage 4 Leaders who do not correctly plan for their Stage 5 transition mistakenly believe that by simply coming to work less often they are properly winding down and transitioning out. They're wrong. "Retiring-on-the-job" isn't Moving On. It's disruptive. That mentality and behavior simply frustrates the team, who now has to wait for the leader to return calls, make decisions, or definitively transfer responsibility to others so the work can continue. Again, most leaders don't see Stage 5 as a leadership step to plan for and through; they view it simply as retiring, quitting, or transitioning careers. However, leadership is about what's right for the organization and the team, not what feels right for the leader. Therefore, successful Stage 5 Leaders focus on the organization and not themselves.

"Retiring on-the-job" isn't Moving On. It's disruptive.

Several years ago, Barry had successfully transitioned out of his leadership role and had turned the reins of his company over to his successor. However, one year later, Barry called to ask me to work with him and his leadership team as they updated their strategic plan.

**"Which team are you talking about?
Have you started a new company?"**

"No. I came back."

"So you made a U-turn?"

"No, not really. I was just hanging around the house with nothing to do. I know how busy things can be here, so I came back to help out and cover some of the projects I used to handle."

"How does the team feel about you being back — really?"

Barry paused, sighed, and then said, "See Liz, this is why I called you. I thought I was calling you to help us update our strategic plan. I told myself if we did that, it would help improve the team's morale. But I have to admit, I don't think everyone's thrilled I came back. I know some of them don't think I trust them to run the company."

"Do you?"

"Do I what?"

"Do you still trust them to run the company? You said you did three years ago when we started this process. Do you still trust them?"

"Yes."

"Have they failed to meet any of their obligations to their customers, vendors, or the bank?"

"No."

"So who are you helping by being back there? You and your need for something to do, or them?"

"Why do I pay you to point out I'm an idiot?"

**"That's my job, remember?
I'm doing my job. Are you doing yours?"**

Be an Effective Stage 5 Leader: Groom Your Successor for Success

As I mentioned when I presented Stage 3 Leadership, a fundamental responsibility for any leader is to ensure the organization is around long after he or she leaves. A crucial piece of that solution is to ensure that you as a Stage 5 Leader have not only backfilled with a leadership team that is effectively doing their jobs, but that you've also helped to identify the individual or individuals who will be taking on your specific roles and responsibilities. In organizations supported by a board of directors, the leadership succession issue is one that should be on their radar screen regularly. A quick way to determine if a board of directors is doing its job is to ask them:

"People don't realize how hard succession is on the incumbent CEO. It's designed to make you able to go away without causing a big impact, and that doesn't come naturally."
—Anne Mulcahy former Xerox CEO

"If something were to happen to the CEO today, who could step in for six months to keep things going? Who could step in as a possible permanent replacement?" Any effective board should be able to answer those questions. If they can't, they're not performing a key responsibility. They're not doing their job.

> *"The final test of a leader is that he leaves behind him in other men the conviction and the will to carry on."*
>
> —*Walter Lippman*

If the board isn't taking on the leadership succession issue, then the organization's owner, CEO, or leader needs to lead that initiative, instead of just supporting it. Even though it will seem odd and might be difficult for many, this is part of the leader's job: to ensure the continued viability and success of the organization through the sound leadership of a capable leader. Who better to help identify the skills, knowledge, character, and insights needed of your successor than you? It is part of your job to identify, either internally or externally, the individual or individuals you believe are best suited to take over your various roles and responsibilities and lead the organization into its future. Then, use your Stage 4 Leadership skills to help them develop the skills and gain the knowledge to step into your roles one step at a time. Even though it may be personally painful, it's right for the organization. The successor(s) become the new "face" of the company. Therefore, they need to speed up as you, the current Stage 5 Leader, start to back out and prepare to move on.

Stage 5 Leaders know in their guts it's time for a change. They know it's time to move on.

Support Key Relationships for Success

As a Stage 5 Leader who plans for and through Stage 5, you'll need to ensure the transition to the new leader or leaders is as seamless as possible. For this to happen, help your successors not only develop their skills, but also develop relationships with the board, senior staff, and other key stakeholders with whom they will work closely. You need to support your successors in earning the trust and respect of others who will be judging them and their potential to take over. Your successors will be responsible for taking over and finalizing various strategic initiatives that you started. Therefore, for their good and for the good of the organization, you'll want to set them up for success.

Leave behind an organization that continues to thrive because of the team you developed. As a Stage 5 Leader, you know that it has always been about the organization. It never was about you.

>> Warning Signs You or One of Your Managers is Having Problems Behaving as a Stage 5 Leader:

- You are not identifying new opportunities outside the organization to share or apply your leadership skills.

- You do not listen to and respond to your own internal need to stay with the organization a bit longer. Therefore, you leave only to end up coming back.

- You do not listen to and respond to your own need to move on. As a result you "retire" on the job.

- You do not provide opportunities to test or gauge the up-and-coming leaders' skills in leading the project, department, or organization before you step away.

- You have not helped to build and bridge professional relationships for your successors to ensure they can more seamlessly transition into these critical roles, responsibilities, relationships, and networks.

- You don't fully trust the new leaders' abilities to work with your former support team to handle the challenges ahead.

If any of these Warning Signs made you un-comfortable, it may be an indication you've not been 'self-less' in supporting or mentoring your successors. A true Stage 5 Leader has only suc-ceeded if the successor succeeds. Stage 5 Leaders keep in the forefront of their thoughts and ac-tions: It's not about me; it's about what is right for the organization. That's what Stage 5 Leaders do.

A true Stage 5 Leader has only succeeded if the successor succeeds.

>> Keys to Stage 5 Leadership:

- Stage 5 Leadership is a transition many don't realize is a focused leadership move. However, it's probably the most selfless move a leader can make.

- Stage 5 Leaders may serve on outside boards to not only share insights and perspectives, but also to gain information on other industries and to further enhance and extend their personal and professional networks.

- Stage 4 Leaders who fail to transition to and through Stage 5 often leave their organizations only to then make a U-turn and return as "the saviors" when they perceive a need.

- Stage 5 is often more difficult than many leaders anticipate, as leaders relinquish their roles, responsibilities, challenges, privileges, and prestige.

- Stage 5 Leaders realize seamless leadership transitions are right for the organization. Therefore, they work to support their successors' successful transition into their new roles.

TRANSITIONING YOUR RESPONSIBILITIES

Leaders — think "Transition"

As you've learned of **The Five Stages of Focused Leadership Development**™, you've seen a consistent theme: You need to transition out of your current role as you support and allow your successor(s) to step in and take over the role and responsibilities.

Regardless of your position, regardless of your title or pay scale, you need to support the smooth transition of your leadership responsibilities. This ensures the work continues to get done efficiently and customers and team members are not negatively impacted by a change in your responsibilities. However, the idea of seamless transitions and succession is missed by many managers. They don't typically think about succession until they start to think about their own retirement or the organization's leadership succession. Yet those are just two types of position succession. Succession occurs any time you transition a

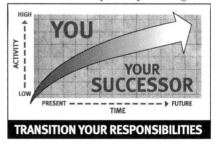

TRANSITION YOUR RESPONSIBILITIES

responsibility to another. Succession and transition need to occur seamlessly at all levels and with all positions in an organization.

Succession occurs any time you transition a responsibility to another.

Thinking about and planning for effective transitions in work responsibilities need to occur at all levels of an organization. Regardless of which stage a leader is in, effective, focused leaders do just that. Stage 1 leaders ensure smooth transitions by developing systems to help successors. Stage 2 leaders ensure smooth transitions by letting go, clarifying expectations, and holding team members accountable. Stage 3 leaders ensure smooth transitions by clarifying and planning for the organization's future. Stage 4 leaders ensure smooth transitions by pushing for the continuous development of talent organization-wide. And Stage 5 leaders ensure smooth transitions by preparing the successor(s) and the team for a new, successful future with new people stepping up to lead the way.

Effective, focused leadership is constantly evolving and changing, depending upon the needs of the team and organization. Effective leaders are in constant transition.

BOARDS OF DIRECTORS

When directors direct and managers manage, incredible things happen.

I have to admit, I am no longer surprised when I hear a board president ask, "So how do we make sure we implement the strategic plan we just completed?" Ironically, I hear this from high-functioning boards, not just ones that are unsure of their responsibilities.

I facilitated the strategic planning process for a highly effective, focused, nonprofit board several years ago. As we were finishing the final work session, JoAnn, the board president and vice president of a hospital system, asked, "Liz, just one more thing — so how do we make sure we implement this plan?" I was stunned. I'd incorrectly interpreted their ability to debate issues strategically and professionally during the work sessions as an indication of their understanding of their role in ensuring the new plan was implemented. So I shared with JoAnn, "That's your job as the board president. Make strategic plan updates a regular part of your quarterly board meetings. Put it on the agenda, then address it. If you don't track it, monitor it, and coordinate with the CEO to make sure action is being taken, who will? Your CEO may or may not. If your strategic plan is not important enough to you, the board, to track and monitor, why bother to develop one in the first place?"

This board's situation was not unique. JoAnn's question was one many boards and board presidents have but don't ask. They're confused because they don't understand what the job of a board and, specifically, a board president is. Boards of directors are supposed to give direction to the president, CEO, or executive director. The boards are supposed to determine strategy based upon their expertise and ability to see the big picture because — now pay attention to this part — they're not supposed to be wrapped up in the day-to-day management issues of the organization. But this is where many boards run into problems. The board president and directors are often too involved in the day-to-day management of the organization. Because many organizations have limited or weak management, many boards get really involved in the operational details and often end up being "doers" and "wannabe managers." **They then stumble over themselves and the "real staff" on who's doing what, and they lose sight of what they're supposed to be doing as a board: determining strategy, monitoring and providing direction to the CEO, tracking** the financials, and planning for leadership succession. Who has time for that when you're determining office reconfigurations with staff?

What is the Board's Job?

The board's role is to advise and direct — through strategic discussion and vote — what path the organization should take in the future. The board discusses and analyzes the big-picture issues that will hinder or allow the organization to grow, achieve its vision, and thrive into the future. To fulfill this responsibility, boards of directors are typically elected by the shareholders or members. In small firms, the boards of directors are often comprised of the business' owners, family members, and select business professionals. In many volunteer and larger organizations, the boards are ideally comprised of select individuals from diverse backgrounds and industries that represent the organization's industry, customer, or membership base — or who can provide needed expertise and insights.

The president, CEO, or executive director (ED) reports to the board. The board of directors has voting power and has full authority to override the decisions of the president or CEO — even if that person founded or owns the company. The board has the authority to hire and fire select key staff — including the president/CEO/ED. A board of directors, through the president/CEO/ED, focuses the actions of the staff and of the organization by developing and approving the strategic plan. The board then holds the president/CEO/ED accountable to ensure the operations are conducted smoothly, effectively, and efficiently as the plan is implemented. The board — which typically only meets once each month or once each quarter — does not have time to debate issues affecting routine operations and non-strategic matters. Boards are supposed to determine strategy to ensure the organization's viability; they're not supposed to be wrapped up in day-to-day management and operational issues.

Boards should do board stuff. Managers should do management stuff. It tends to work better that way.

However, this becomes a challenge for many board members, as they are currently CEOs or leaders of other organizations. As such, they tend to get involved in the operational and management issues because that's what they do in their "real" jobs. They resolve management issues regularly in their own organizations, so it's relatively easy and tempting for a board member or members to jump in and take on select management or senior staff duties — just to help get things done. Effective board members need to remember this is acceptable and expected in exceptional cases. However, their real job as board members is to provide direction to the management staff, not do its work. The board members need to operate in Stages 3, 4, and 5 — Leading, Mentoring, and coordinating the Moving On activities — not Doing or Managing.

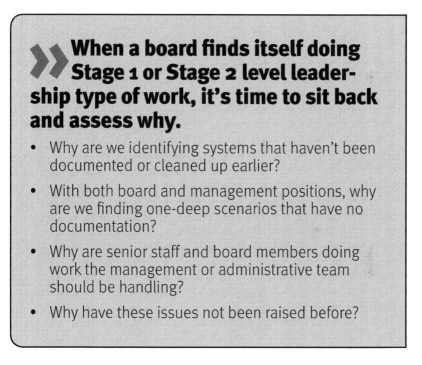

>> When a board finds itself doing Stage 1 or Stage 2 level leadership type of work, it's time to sit back and assess why.

- Why are we identifying systems that haven't been documented or cleaned up earlier?

- With both board and management positions, why are we finding one-deep scenarios that have no documentation?

- Why are senior staff and board members doing work the management or administrative team should be handling?

- Why have these issues not been raised before?

The point of this board versus management roles review is not to place blame, but to identify the problem so it can be resolved. There may well be changes needed in the way the board conducts itself, how it treats the management staff, or what it expects of staff. Whatever the problems and subsequent actions steps needed to resolve deficiencies, the board and management staff need to discuss, plan, and address them together. Then the board can focus on advising, and the management team can focus on managing.

"Boards that don't put into place a strong succession plan will continue to get the CEOs they deserve."
—A.G. Lafley, former CEO and Chairman of Proctor & Gamble

>>Therefore, for a board to do its job, it needs to:

- Let management do its job. The board members need to stay out of the day-to-day operational issues.

- Remember, the management team works for the board. The board doesn't work for management. If the board members are doing things the managers should be doing, it's time to stop and clarify roles, responsibilities, boundaries, and expectations.

- Have strong management in place to handle the management issues effectively so the board can focus on board issues.

If the board focuses its time and efforts to more effectively fulfill its responsibilities, by default more legwork and management accountability is pushed to the management team.

When directors direct and managers manage, incredible things happen in organizations. It just requires work, focus, and a willingness to be responsible and accountable to do your job.

Plan for Succession Success

This discussion of board responsibilities wouldn't be complete without specifically addressing succession planning in organizations. Planning for leadership succession is a fundamental responsibility of the board. However, according a 2016 study by Norwich, over 50 percent of companies with revenues of $500 million or more do not have a proper CEO succession plan in place. Also, 78 percent of nonprofits could not immediately name a successor. Those are sobering statistics.

Leadership succession is more than simply filling open or soon-to-be-open slots. Leadership succession is more than identifying the "Hot Spots" and one-deep scenarios. Leadership succession is about finding the right people with the right talent at the right time to move the position, department, or organization forward.

When directors direct and managers manage, incredible things happen in organizations. It just requires work, focus, and a willingness to be responsible and accountable to do your job.

But here's the key: Finding the right people takes time, and especially so when you're looking for the organization's future CEO.

That's why effective Stage 4 Leaders focus on identifying, acquiring or developing, and mentoring talent constantly. Effective Stage 4 Leaders realize their job is to keep building that talent pool with the right talent for the organization's future. Effective boards need to push for and support Stage 4 Leadership. It's right for the organization's future; therefore, it's right for the board to address.

▶▶ Warning Signs Your Board is Failing to do its Job:

- There are no successor(s) for critical positions identified, nor is there a process in place to identify one.

- Board meeting time is spent on operational, day-to-day management issues, instead of strategic issues to ensure the viability and relevance of the organization.

- The president/CEO/executive director regularly brings operational and management issues to the board to resolve — and they do.

- Board members are performing management functions (i.e., managing departments, projects, and staff).

- Board members circumvent the president/CEO/ED and interact directly and frequently with various staff.

If your board is experiencing any of these Warning Signs, it's time to act. It's time to clarify the board's role and responsibilities and those of the management team.

Effective boards support their managers and leadership team. The most effective way of supporting them is by not doing their jobs for them or getting in their way. Directors direct. Managers manage. Effective boards do this.

⟫ Key Points for Boards:

- The role of the board of directors is to advise and direct — through policy discussion and vote — what direction the organization should take in the future.

- Boards are supposed to determine strategy to ensure the organization's viability; they're not supposed to be wrapped up in day-to-day management and operational issues.

- The board hires and fires select key staff — including the president/CEO/executive director.

- The board members need to operate in Stages 3, 4, and 5: Leading, Mentoring, and Moving On — not Doing or Managing.

- Boards should support management's Stage 4 Leadership efforts by identifying, developing, and mentoring talent continuously for the long-term good of the organization.

- Effective Stage 4 Leaders realize their job is to keep building the talent pool with the right talent for the organization's future. Effective boards support this.

SECTION 2

FOR INDIVIDUAL REFERENCE AND SELF-REFLECTION:

"START BY DOING WHAT'S NECESSARY;
THEN DO WHAT'S POSSIBLE;
AND SUDDENLY YOU ARE DOING
THE IMPOSSIBLE."
—ST. FRANCIS OF ASSISI

What Type of Leader Does Your Organization and Team Need?

The Five Stages of
Focused Leadership Development™

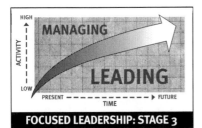

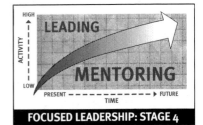

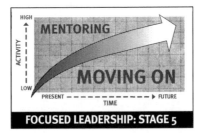

Leaders move among the various stages each day. But effective leaders move among the right stages at the right times.

This insight needs to be a gut-level understanding. You can't effectively move up to the next stage of leadership yourself until your current stage leadership skills are solid and are being developed in your team members so they can take over as you move on. Remember: Backfill to move on.

You need to be the type of leader they need you to be so they can progress. As an effective leader, you know: It's about them, not you.

As I shared **The Five Stages of Focused Leadership Development**™, did you see yourself at various times in many of them? If you did, that's normal — and good. On any day, you should be moving among the five stages depending upon the project or people with whom you are working. To be an effective leader, you need to flex and move depending upon the needs of your team and your organization. You need to be the type of leader they need you to be so they can progress. As an effective leader, you know; It's about them, not you.

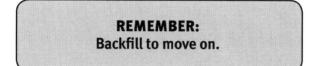

REMEMBER:
Backfill to move on.

If you have not yet taken your free Five Stages Leadership Assessment, go to www.WBSLLC.com *and take it now!*

Are You Moving Among the Right Stages?

Leaders move among the various stages each day. But effective leaders move among the right stages at the right times. This insight needs to be a gut-level understanding. You can't effectively move up to the next stage of leadership yourself until your current stage leadership skills are solid and are being developed in your team members so they can take over as you move on. **Remember: Backfill to move on.**

For instance, you may think you're ready to call yourself a Stage 3 Leader, but you're not if your team members and managers are still bringing the bulk of their problems to you to solve. Unless your team members themselves are operating at Stage 2, you can't operate at a Stage 3 Leadership level (i.e., you can't lead until you've taught others how to manage). If your team needs help learning how to operate in Stage 2, operate in Stage 2 Leadership mode yourself to support their Stage 2 development. Model the behavior you need them to develop. Coach and teach them the specific skills and actions you are modeling as a Stage 2 Leader that they need to develop and demonstrate. Then as they develop stronger Stage 2 Leadership skills, you can start to move yourself more into Stage 3.

Perhaps your team is developed to the point of allowing you to operate at Stage 4 Leadership most of the time. However, with the introduction of a new company-wide strategic initiative, you will want to step back into Stage 1 Leadership behaviors as you need to be involved with the initial project strategy discussions and debates. Your insights are crucial to clarifying with the project team the project's impact on the organization, its impact on tangent departments and systems, and the necessary project deliverables. However, you quickly move into Stage 2 as the project team starts to independently perform in Stage 1 while they debate and develop the new processes and protocols. Next, as the project team becomes more skilled and confident in implementing the project, you support their transition into more Stage 2 level activities as you move on to Stage 3. Finally, you move back to Stage 4 as the project team demonstrates Stage 3 thinking by anticipating and planning for future enhancements to the project.

On the other hand, you may be completely happy operating as a Stage 2 Leader. In fact, you're such a good Stage 2 Leader, you've helped develop several strong Stage 2 Leaders on your team. So it's time to move on, right? But what if you don't want to move on? That's fine. Then you need to support the advancement of another team member. The team needs a Stage 3 Leader now. If that leader is not going to be you, let go and support the advancement of the team member who has the right Stage 3 Leadership skills for the team.

> **If you don't want to move on — fine. Then you need to let go and support the advancement of another team member who has the leadership skills the team needs.**

In order for an organization's strategic projects to morph and evolve, the leadership needs to grow, evolve, and let go. As I've said before, the key is to ensure you are leading from the stage your team and organization needs so they can progress.

If you don't let go, others can't do. It's a repeating theme. It's part of a growth cycle at each stage of leadership for each stage of your team's and individual team member's development. To be effective at each stage, you've had to first learn the necessary skills, behaviors, and thought patterns yourself. You practiced, adapted, and ultimately became proficient at them at each stage. As you gained skills, you shared them with your team members to develop their skills as well. As you enhanced your skills, you helped to enhance theirs. You backfilled. Now someone needs to move on.

"Leadership should be more participative than directive, more enabling than performing."
—Mary D. Poole

In Which Stage Should You Operate?

So now you know you need to change the way you've been leading. But what should you be doing? In which stage should you operate most often?

Who Should Operate in Stage 1?

FOCUSED LEADERSHIP: STAGE 1

Most Often: Front-line employees — Doers — with leadership potential who want to simplify, organize, and improve operations.

Often: New supervisors who are expected to continue to also produce or fill in when staff are out and perform as Doers to ensure production is met.

As Needed: Team leaders, supervisors, and managers who have a specific technical expertise needed to perform specific tasks (i.e., prepare budgets, review plans, design programs or processes, etc.)

As Needed: Managers and leaders whose experience, perspective, and authority are needed to help kick off a new strategic project or initiative.

Who Should Operate in Stage 2?

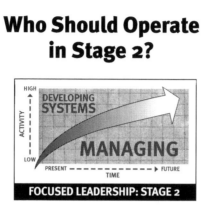

Most Often: New supervisors of a team (inherited or created) who need to clarify every team member's role and responsibilities — starting with the new supervisor's.

Most Often: Team leaders, supervisors, and managers who need to backfill specific skills and expertise in others to build depth and ensure others can step in and keep things moving while the team leader/supervisor/manager is away.

Often: Front-line employees — Doers — with demonstrated leadership potential who coach and train peers and lead projects.

Often: Managers and leaders who need to develop management thinking, organizational insights, and skills in others, so they can take over the project management responsibilities.

Who Should Operate in Stage 3?

FOCUSED LEADERSHIP: STAGE 3

Often: Managers and leaders who are responsible for ensuring the organization is viable and successful three, four, five, to ten or more years into the future. Managers and leaders who need to be asking themselves: In spite of all of our current operational challenges, what do we need to focus on next to ensure our future? What's next for us, and how do we make that happen?

As Needed: Front-line veteran doers with demonstrated leadership thinking who can provide specific front-line insights and impacts of potential strategic projects and initiatives.

As Needed: Team leaders, supervisors, and managers who need to clarify their department, project, or work area's role in fulfilling the organization's vision and identifying, specifically, what their teams need to do next to make the vision a reality.

Who Should Operate in Stage 4?

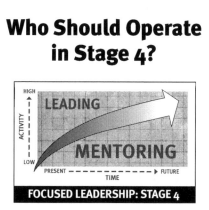

Most Often: Managers and leaders who recognize the gap in the skills and knowledge of their current team members and the skills and knowledge their teams will need in the future.

As Needed: Front-line, veteran doers with demonstrated leadership skills who have spent a great deal of time doing what they do, have been instrumental in developing many of the current systems, but who also share their knowledge with others to help newer doers learn to perform proficiently.

As Needed: Team leaders, supervisors, and managers who need to help newer staff and team members understand not only the overt workings of the organization, but the subtle nuances of how and why things are the way they are.

Who Should Operate in Stage 5?

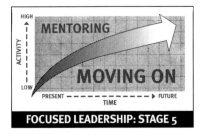

FOCUSED LEADERSHIP: STAGE 5

Always: Any team member or leader who will be transitioning a role, responsibility, or position. Every transition should be seamless.

As Needed: Senior managers and leaders who know they themselves are planning to move on to a new job, new organization, or new phase of life.

As Needed: Front-line veteran doers with demonstrated leadership skills who are planning to move on to a new job, new organization, or new phase of life within the next few weeks to 12 months. Veteran doers need to plan for their departure to help ensure seamless transitions.

As Needed: Team leaders, supervisors, and managers who know they themselves or one of their team members is planning to move on to a new job, new organization, or new phase of life within the next six to 12 months. Team leaders, supervisors, and managers need to plan for their own or a team member's departure to help facilitate seamless transitions and to ensure that backfilling has occurred.

*Which stage
do you operate in
most often?
In which stage are
you operating?*

SECTION 3

ASSESSMENTS, TRAINING KIT AND MORE

"WE CANNOT CHANGE WHAT
WE ARE NOT AWARE OF,
AND ONCE WE ARE AWARE,
WE CANNOT HELP BUT CHANGE."
—SHERYL SANDBERG

Because, like you, so many leaders have found The Five Stages of Focused Leadership Development™ so powerful and effective, we've developed additional tools to help you leverage this model and its insights even more!

FREE Templates and Other Tools

Go to **www.WBSLLC.com/5-stages** for your free templates and other tools to help you become the leader your team needs you to be!

FREE Leadership Stage Assessment

I've mentioned this a few times already, but if you haven't yet taken the FREE Five Stages Leadership Assessment to identify your current stage of leadership, don't wait any longer! **Just go to www.WBSLLC.com and click the orange triangle!** ▲

Group Assessments & Group Reports

The REAL power of the assessment comes into play when your ENTIRE leadership team takes the assessment. When the entire team participates, you're able to quickly identify which stage(s) of Focused Leadership Development your team needs to address.

- Your team's customized report provides not only a team overview, but a person-by-person breakdown of each team member's current stage of leadership behavior.
- This enables you to provide focused coaching to team members to help them — and their teams — move forward.

▶▶ Go to www.WBSLLC.com/Assessments for information

Team and Group Discussion Questions

To get the most out of this book, share the ideas with others. Use it to kick off a discussion of your team's leadership challenges and management frustrations. Use it to pinpoint commonalities and areas of focus for your team. Use it as a resource to help bring your team together to discuss, debate, share, and grow.

- The following Section provides over 25 suggested discussion questions to help you, your board, your team, or book club dive deeper into each of the Five Stages.
- Select just one discussion question to start a leadership team meeting to get people thinking, talking, and collaborating.

Train The Trainer I Training Kits

Would you like to DIY — do it yourself — and facilitate training and conversations around this book and
The Five Stages of Focused Leadership Development™?

Would you like to be a key player in developing
your company's leadership skills?

GREAT!

》》 Go to www.WBSLLC.com/Five-Stages-Trainers for information on how you can bring this program into your organization

Do you want to share these resources with your entire team or group?
Call +1(717)597-8890 for information on bulk order discounts!

161

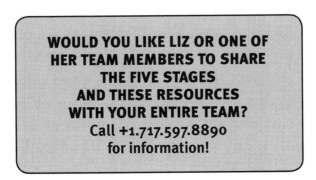

WOULD YOU LIKE LIZ OR ONE OF
HER TEAM MEMBERS TO SHARE
THE FIVE STAGES
AND THESE RESOURCES
WITH YOUR ENTIRE TEAM?
Call +1.717.597.8890
for information!

SECTION 4

FOR MANAGEMENT TEAMS AND BOOK CLUBS:

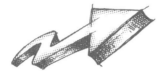

"SUCCESS DOESN'T REQUIRE MONEY.
IT REQUIRES DISCIPLINE."
—LIZ WEBER

Group Discussion Questions for Deeper Learning and Application

• • •

These discussion questions are shared with the hope that management teams and book clubs will find them not only thought-provoking, but genuinely helpful in changing the way they lead.

Please use these discussion questions during:

» Book Club gatherings
» Master Mind work sessions
» Brown Bag Lunches
» Staff meetings
» Internal leadership training programs
» Leadership team meetings
» Leadership Retreats
» Board of Director Retreats
» Other gatherings intended to spur thought, discussion, self-reflection, team-building, and excitement.

Thanks for reading the book.
Now enjoy the questions and conversations that will follow!

Overview and General Kick-Off Program
Questions & Activities:

1. What is your **real** job?

    a: What does your team expect you to do?

    b: What do your colleagues expect you to do?

    c: What does your boss expect you to do?

    d: What do your customers expect you to do?

2. How much of your time, at your hourly rate, is wasted each year because you are doing work others are being paid to do?

3. What are some specific changes your team would realize if you and your team members all operated at the appropriate Stage 1–5 levels when needed?

4. Which of The Five Stages of Focused Leadership Development™ do you see yourself operating in now?

    a: Why?

5. What do you need to change in how you are leading?

Stage 1 Discussion Questions:

1. What types of problems do others bring to you to solve?

2. As you learned about Stage 1 Leadership, what specific systems, processes, or procedures do you or your team work through or work around that need to be documented, reviewed, or updated?

3. Where do you see duplication or redundancies in systems and processes you or your team use?

4. When you go on vacation, are you able to step away from work and relax, knowing others are covering your key tasks, or are you regularly communicating with your customers and colleagues to keep the work moving?

5. What do you need to change in how you are leading?

Stage 2 Discussion Questions:

1. Why isn't your team as productive as it could be?

2. What types of problems do your team members bring to you to solve?

3. As a manager, how do you "Let Go" and initially let production numbers drop and errors rise while the Doers learn to do the work they're being paid to do?

4. What tasks do you need to stop doing so your team members can start doing them?

5. If you don't address unacceptable behaviors, you get what you allow. What bad behaviors have you allowed team members and team members you inherited to continue?

6. What do you need to change in how you are leading?

Stage 3 Discussion Questions:

1. How well do you understand your current strategic plan?

2. What will your customers of the future need you to provide?

3. What do you need to have in place 3, 4, or 5 or more years from now to ensure your organization's viability and relevance?

4. Do your team members each know how they fit in and matter?

5. How effective have you been at intentionally creating time to think and plan strategically?

6. What do you need to change in how you are leading?

Stage 4 Discussion Questions:

1. What has occurred or may be occurring that might indicate the management and leadership team's skills are over-extended?

    a: What are you doing to address this?

    b: What do you need to do to mitigate this from happening in the future?

2. Where do you have known "Hot Spots" within your team?

    a: What are you doing to address this?

3. What systems, processes, and procedures, developed in Stage 1, can you now use to support cross-training to create greater depth?

4. What is being done to develop talent deep and wide within your organization?

5. What do you need to change in how you are leading?

Stage 5 Discussion Questions:

1. What types of problems do you try to ensure your successor can resolve?

2. What specifically have you done or do you do to ensure transitions are seamless?

3. What have been indicators to you that it's time for you to move on from a project, team, or organization?

4. What issues arise when a team member or colleague retires on the job?

5. As you anticipate "Moving On" to a new task, project, position, organization, or stage in life, how do you change how you're leading to transition as seamlessly as possible?

Board of Directors Discussion Questions:

1. What types of problems does the staff bring to you to solve?

2. What process is in place to ensure there are successors lined-up or identified to fill critical positions?

3. How do you keep the board meetings focused on strategic, board-level issues, and not focused on operational, staff-level issues?

4. What happens when board members take on management functions?

5. What happens when board members circumvent the president/CEO/executive director and manage staff directly?

6. What do you do to ensure all board members are clear on their role and responsibilities?

7. What needs to change in how you are leading?

Stop by www.WBSLLC.com for your FREE FIVE STAGES LEADERSHIP ASSESSMENT!

Wrapping Up

Being a manager or a leader is a privilege. It's an honor to have others respect your abilities enough to allow you to lead them. It's an honor to have others trust you to guide them and support them as you work together. The roles and responsibilities of management and leadership are difficult, stressful, and can be terribly frustrating. However, by clearly understanding what your real job as a leader is, and then doing that job, you'll be more effective, and you'll be able to help your teams become more successful too.

So if you're ready to get your life back, do your job — your real job. Someone needs to change around here…**you.**

*So if you're ready to get your life back, do your job — your real job. Someone needs to change around here…***you.**

CONTINUE YOUR LEADERSHIP JOURNEY WITH THESE PRODUCTS BY LIZ WEBER
Available at WBSLLC.com/Store

STOP SO YOU CAN GET THE RESULTS YOU WANT

In this set of four books, Liz takes you by the hand and tells you what you need to Stop doing and what you need to Start doing to realize the leadership success you want!

Each book contains ten thought-provoking and business-changing insights. Buy them separately or as a set:

- **What Business Owners Need to Stop Doing**
- **What Managers Need to Stop Doing**
- **What Human Resources Professionals Need to Stop Doing**
- **What Women in Leadership Need to Stop Doing**

DON'T LET 'EM TREAT YOU LIKE A GIRL® — A WOMAN'S GUIDE TO LEADERSHIP SUCCESS

With insights gathered from women and men in leadership roles, Liz shares tips to help aspiring to experienced women leaders.

This quick-reading, insightful guide helps you identify:

- Which leadership traits are most admired
- What your leadership brand is saying about you
- How to manage conflicts and negotiations more effectively
- What "girly" behaviors you need to STOP!

This is a great resource for Women's Leadership programs!

Video Series:
STRATEGIC PLANNING WITHOUT THE MIGRAINE!™

In this six-session video series, you will be guided through Liz's Success Planning Pyramid™ process of strategic planning. Liz shares numerous examples and tips to help you develop a solid, workable, focused plan – without the migraine! A great resource for small businesses and non-profits!

This series shares how to:

- **Create a Clear Strategic Plan:** How to Keep it Simple & Aligned
- **Conduct a SWOT Analysis:** Identify Your Realities & Opportunities
- **Clarify Your Mission:** Why Do You Exist?
- **Determine Your Vision:** What Does Your Future Look Like?
- **Create Your Values:** What Are Your House Rules?
- **Create Goals to Make "It" Happen:** What Do You Need to Do – Specifically?

Why not bring the power and insights in this book to your group or team?

Liz provides content-rich, interactive, skill-building presentations to groups large and small.
Liz is known for her candor and her ability to customize her topics to meet your group's specific needs.

About the Author **Liz Weber**

In the words of one client, "Liz Weber will help you see opportunities you never knew existed."

Known for her candor, clear insights, and straightforward approach, Liz Weber is a sought-after strategic leadership expert, executive coach, and speaker. She is one of fewer than 100 people in the U.S. to hold both the Certified Speaking Professional (CSP) and Certified Management Consultant (CMC) designations – the highest earned designations in two different professions.

As experts in strategic planning, succession planning, and leadership development, Liz and her team are based near Harrisburg, Pennsylvania, and work with leaders to take their organizations:

- From no business strategy to enterprise-wide focus and clarity
- From no succession or workforce plan to enterprise-wide depth
- From a weak leadership team to a respected leadership team

Liz has supervised business activities in 139 countries and has consulted with organizations in over 20 countries. She has designed and facilitated conferences from Bangkok to Bonn and

Tokyo to Tunis. Liz has taught for the Johns Hopkins University's Graduate School of Continuing Studies, as well as the Georgetown University's Senior Executive Leadership Program.

Liz is also the author of nine leadership publications including:
  » *Stop So You Can Get the Results You Want*
  » *Don't Let 'Em Treat You Like a Girl—A Woman's Guide to Leadership Success* 1st–3rd Editions (2004, 2006, and 2011)

Liz's *Manager's Corner* column appears monthly in several trade publications, association newsletters, and internet resource centers for executives.

Why not bring the power and insights in this book to your group or team? Liz provides content-rich, interactive, skill-building presentations to groups large and small. Liz is known for her candor and her ability to customize her topics to meet your group's specific needs.

This book is available from Amazon.com in print and for Kindle.

For more information on Liz, her services and leadership resources, go to www.WBSLLC.com or www.Liz-Weber.com

Twitter @LizWeberCMC
Facebook LizWeberCMC
LinkedIn LizWeberCMC

50339278R00108

Made in the USA
Middletown, DE
29 June 2019